Ugly Dog Sweaters and Other Indignities

A collection of fun and heartwarming stories from

Keke's Guide to Training Your Human

Keke

and Ken Van Camp

Dedication

I dedicate this book to my dear friend and fellow dog enthusiast, Chris Kinstler, whose friendship and sense of humor always bring a smile to my face. You helped rekindle my love for Peter Mayle's writing, whose vignettes from his "Provence" series of books, rich with wit and evocative detail, were a model and inspiration for many of Keke's stories.

Thank you for championing Keke's adventures, even when they veered into her mischievous "Tripod" phase. Your unwavering support means the world.

Acknowledgments

I am deeply grateful to my critique group, Writers of The Villages South, for their invaluable feedback, ideas, and inspiration throughout this journey.

My sincere thanks also go to the Writer's League of The Villages, Pen, Paper and Pals, Wine and Words, the Florida Writers Association, and the Dynamic Dog Club of The Villages. Your collective wisdom and camaraderie have been instrumental in my growth as a writer.

To my friends, family, fellow dog owners, and writers—your encouragement has been a constant source of motivation.

A heartfelt thank you to my faithful followers on Medium and Substack. Your weekly readership, likes, claps, and insightful comments have meant the world to me.

I am especially indebted to my beta readers: Jody Perkins, John Boggess, Barbara Rein, Rick and Kim Rozelle, and Bill Hurst. Your thorough feedback was crucial in refining this manuscript.

The love and support from all these wonderful individuals gave me the confidence to write this book. Thank you for being part of this journey.

Credits

Cover design by James Kayode.

Photo of Lassie and Jeff Miller in It Takes a Thief public domain from Wikimedia Commons

Photo of dog walking in How to Keep Your Human in Shape by Delphine Beausoleil from Unsplash

Photo of Chinese Crested in Finding Your Dream Job by ivabalk from Pixabay

Photo of bullseye in The Bird Poop Chronicles (Part 1) by Julian Hochgesang from Unsplash

Photo of beer can in When the Breeze Turned Bitter by Brian Yurasits on Unsplash

Photo of Get out of jail free card in The Next Stop (Part 2 of Vacation Getaways) from Wikimedia Creative Commons

Photo of Keke looking from behind plate in Dog On It (Part 3 of Vacation Getaways) by Amanda Henderson

Photo of scarecrow in grey dress in Dog On It (Part 3 of Vacation Getaways) by Xianyu hao from Unsplash

Photo of Zoey sleeping in Happy Father's Day From the Cat by Amanda Henderson

Photo of Golden retriever standing over a long-haired Shih-Tsu in Shear Madness by Jeyakumaran Mayooresan from Unsplash

Photo of dog with tennis ball in Takin' Care of Business by Victoria Orozco from Unsplash

All photos in The Wizard Will See You Now used with permission from Bionic Pets LLC

Table of Contents

Introduction from Ken (aka "Keke's more trainable human").... 9

It Takes a Thief 11

Does Your Stuffed Toy Really Stand a Chance Against Hannibal Lecter? 15

A New Maneuver in Olympic Tennis................................ 21

Pawprints in the Concrete 25

Broken? But You Said I Was Perfect! 29

The Phone Ate My Human's Brain................................. 35

Happy National Puppy Day 41

How to Keep Your Human in Shape 45

Finding Your Dream Job 51

Understanding Human Packs 59

The Bird Poop Chronicles (Part 1) 63

The Bird Poop Chronicles (Conclusion) 71

The Ultimate Alarm Clock.. 75

Sometimes You Have to Poop in the House 79

Paradin' o' the Green 83

When the Breeze Turned Bitter................................... 85

Learning Dog Tricks 89

The Headbangers Ball 95

Happy Birthday, Keke! 99

I'm Not So Hot About Growing Up 103

At the Lake (Part 1 of Vacation Getaways) 107

The Next Stop (Part 2 of Vacation Getaways)................... 113

Dog On It (Part 3 of Vacation Getaways)....................... 117

Building Character (Conclusion of Vacation Getaways)...... 123

Happy Father's Day From the Cat............................... 127

Shear Madness 131

Being Ghosted 135

Ugly Dog Sweaters and Other Indignities 141

Takin' Care of Business 145

The Buddy System 149

Reading Doggish 157

The Wizard Will See You Now 165

Tempus Fugit.. 173

Are You Ready for Sweet Little Teddy? (Part 1) 177

UFOs Over New Jersey... 185

Are You Ready for Sweet Little Teddy? (Conclusion) 191

What the World Needs Now Is Love.................................... 199

Traveling the Not-So-Friendly Skies 203

Baby Burrito: No Fur. No Tail. No Sleep. 209

Conclusion 215

Introduction from Ken
(aka "Keke's more trainable human")

Congratulations—you're owned by a dog! That fluffy ball of playful innocence is gazing at you with adoring eyes. She (or he) is lovable, cuddly, and so, so charming.

Just think: soon, whenever you return home, you'll be greeted by your new best friend, tail wagging, thrilled to see you, eager to show off how well they've behaved.

- - Insert lengthy record scratch sound here. - -

Just kidding! Now let me tell you how this really works.

Welcome to the underworld of canines, where every yip is a negotiation, every head tilt is a calculated ploy, and every nap is merely a tactical retreat in their ongoing war for household dominance. Sure, they're adorable—but that's part of the master plan. Beneath that innocent exterior lies a cunning strategist with one primary mission: identify the alpha in your house... and dethrone them.

If puppies were as angelic as they appear, *Keke's Guide to Training Your Human* would not exist. This book is based on that popular blog and is the second collection of bite-sized lessons from Keke herself. In her first book, *The Dog Park Massacre*, Keke served up more than forty of her insights into the art of human training, and this book continues, presenting fresh wisdom from that tiny renegade.

My wife and I adopted Keke when she was three months old, and at the time of this writing, Keke is nearing her second birthday. I often look at her and wonder, "What on Earth could she be thinking?" And it's still a joy to wake up in the morning and find those dark, soulful eyes staring at me, apparently saying, "I've got you. You're my human." As long as that wonderful, frustrating relationship continues between human and master, I'll continue writing her stories.

So, grab a snack for yourself (and a treat or two for your canine overlord), snuggle up with your furry friend, and prepare to learn a thing or two about the real ruler of your home.

As Keke would say: "If you can't beat 'em, stock up on treats and prepare for a life of joyful servitude."

Ken Van Camp

It Takes a Thief

What's a Little Larceny Between Friends?

Wolves do not always hunt in packs. Sometimes, a lone wolf must rely on her own cunning.

Silent as a shadow, I creep through the grass, every muscle primed for the perfect strike. Patience is my greatest weapon.

With lightning speed, I lunge. My captive never stood a chance. My sharp fangs sink into the soft white underbelly—victory is mine!

"Keke, what did you do to my tissue?" Mommy asks.

The ferocious wolf retreats, dragging the shredded trophy to her den, where the spoils of her conquest soon lie scattered like snowflakes in a blizzard. Mommy follows.

"Or, more to the point, what did my poor tissue ever do to you?"

The wide-eyed wolf wags her tail, lowers her head to the ground, and looks up with a contrite but defiant glint in her eyes.

It dared to exist in my territory, and now it's mine.

I wag a little harder.

Can we call it a decorative improvement?

Mommy sighs. "It's a good thing you're so cute—or you'd be a throw pillow by now."

I am not the first canine to execute a flawless heist and walk away with my tail wagging. Oh no, my escapade is part of a proud legacy of infamous doggy larcenists.

Take Buddy from *Air Bud*, for instance. He didn't just steal a basketball—he stole the game, the glory, and the crowd's hearts, all without so much as a foul called.

And don't forget Lassie, the queen of canine kleptomania. She pilfered ropes, tools, and probably a few other things that never made it on camera, all under the noble pretense of saving Timmy from another well.

Then there's Hooch from *Turner and Hooch*, a master thief of an entirely different kind. He didn't just steal snacks—he stole scenes, screen time, and even Tom Hanks' spotlight.

But the greatest heist of all time? That was the one my Momma taught me. No, not my human "Mommy"—I mean my first Momma, the one who gave me life and an unbeatable strategy for winning humans over.

She coached me on what to do when prospective companions visited my breeder. "First," she said, "engage them in play. Keep it classy—no jumping or slobbering on their shoes. That'll get them to sit on the floor with you. Any toy will do—ball, rope, maybe even the corner of a shoe if you're feeling daring."

"Next," she continued, "when they're fully invested, let out the tiniest little yip. Just one. Not too loud— you're not a car alarm. Get ready for the grand finale, your Oscar moment."

She explained it all: limp ever so slightly, just enough to raise concern, and climb gingerly into their lap. Make eye contact—a deep, soulful stare. Lock eyes like your future depends on it because, frankly, it does. Hold their gaze until you sense their defenses crumbling.

Then deliver the coup de grâce: make yourself impossibly small. Curl into a tiny ball like you've just deflated from all the cuteness. Close your eyes and exhale a little ragged sigh—the kind that says, "I've found my forever home, and I'm already dreaming of it."

And that's it. That's how you pull off the ultimate heist. You walk away with the most precious treasure of all: their hearts.

Does Your Stuffed Toy Really Stand a Chance Against Hannibal Lecter?

There's a fine line between aspiring surgeon and cannibalistic killer

Dogs love stuffed toys. Why?

To understand our true intentions, let me tell you a story about a stuffed squirrel I received from friends. We'll name our squirrel, "Rocky."

Humans think they're giving dogs cute, fun toys that will lead to years of engaging playtime. As you will see, we have somewhat different objectives for our new fluffy friend.

A new stuffed toy undergoes four phases in its lifetime. First, there is the unwrapping—a fun, crunchy phase that results in a pile of shredded paper from the display packaging. I've previously written about the ecstasy of unwrapping presents in Book One, so I'll skip these details for now.

Rocky the squirrel is cute and mostly brown. He has a couple of black stripes down his back and a fuzzy tail nearly as long as his body. His head has two ears, two eyes, and a little smirk on his mouth with no better purpose than to taunt me.

Once the toy has been liberated from its packaging, my two-legged gift giver often wants to engage me in the second phase, a game of "fetch." Since I appreciate the thought and caring that went into the present, I'm happy to oblige and engage in this bit of frivolity before getting down to business.

Just one of the many sacrifices I make to keep my humans content. I can only do so much.

The fetching phase is usually followed by a third "tug toy" phase in which my benefactor has fun trying to take Rocky away from me, so she can throw the toy again and prolong the game of fetch. This may last for a few throws before the human becomes distracted by the latest viral TikTok video, a notification from her Ring camera, or the carriage scene from Season 3 of Bridgerton.

At this point, we progress to the fourth phase—the one nature intended for our dear fluffy rodent—that of "chew toy." Since I have now been left alone with my new squirrelly friend, it is time to put my forensic talents to the test.

I usually begin with the largest and most annoying extremity, which, in Rocky's case, is his bushy tail. I may start by testing for a poorly attached appendage by holding down his body with my paws and pulling the tail vigorously with my teeth. A well-constructed and dog-friendly toy will present a good fight here, and in Rocky's case, I was not disappointed.

Although Rocky's tail stayed attached to his body, I succeeded in dislodging several strands of fur. Experimentation revealed the optimal chewing angle and the best teeth to apply, so in short order, I removed most of the fur from one side of his hind part.

Bowels in or bowels out?

The "chew toy" phase can be further broken down into sub-phases, such as the "no witnesses" phase (in which the eyes are chewed off), the "denuding" phase, the "organ donation" phase, the "wipe that smug little smirk off his face" phase, and finally the "I can't remember anymore what this toy was originally, but it's still tasty" phase.

Most of the sub-phases speak for themselves, but none speak louder than the organ donation phase—especially when the organ happens to be a squeaker. Its extraction is one of the most satisfying accomplishments for any animal, but it must be approached with caution.

First of all, if you squeak the toy too many times while trying to extricate the organ, it could draw attention from your humans. This is especially likely if the humans are engaged in an activity where they are sensitive to excessive noises, such as when napping, practicing Yoga, or listening to the dulcet tones of a Sandals Resort ad on TV.

"One love, one love…"

Mommy? Are you with us, Mommy?

It's okay, she's somewhere on a Caribbean island. Squeak as much as you like.

Secondly, you want to squirrel away the squeaker in a convenient hiding place where you can return to that miniature whoopee cushion when most needed. When the humans are all gone, for instance, and you're looking for a fun way to annoy the family cat.

And lastly, of course, the squeaker will need further dissection of its own. The gift that keeps on giving, as they say.

Before you so-called "expert dog dieticians" get all up in my snout about the dangers of ingesting non-food items, let's talk about how humans have an unnaturally narrow—and wildly hypocritical—definition of "food." One minute, you're scolding me for eating the stuffing out of a chew toy, and the next, you're popping cheese puffs like they're hand-delivered by the Treat Fairy herself.

Here, I must pause and point out that small plastic toys like squeakers are dangerous if consumed by any animal (or small child). They have the potential to be a choking hazard or could cause intestinal blockage and should, therefore, be taken away and properly discarded in the trash.

There. I said it. I didn't want to say it, but the lawyers insisted on it. What a way to ruin a beautiful ending to a story. It's like those happy drug commercials that end with an auctioneer's voice running through all the possible side effects, including bowel perforation, necrosis, malnutrition, and death. Nothing to lose any sleep over, right?

And so we come to the end of our triumphant story. That time when we attempt to name our luscious and generous toy formerly known as "Rocky." Perhaps we could now call him "The Stuffingless Stallion," or maybe "Battered Balboa, the One-Eyed Champ." Write and let me know your preferred moniker for our newly redesigned toy.

A New Maneuver in Olympic Tennis

You've got skills.
Make sure you get proper credit for them.

I love watching the Olympics on TV, and earlier this month, I caught the pre-trials for the U.S. gymnastics team. Simone Biles does jumps and twists that make Deadpool and Wolverine look like they're taking a nap. She even has a new move named after her—the "Biles 2."

Really? That's the best they could come up with?

This from the species that invented *Cherry Garcia* and *Chunky Monkey*?

Personally, I think her move should be renamed *Spider-Biles*. What do you think?

Another Olympic sport I enjoy is tennis. It's more fun to play than gymnastics, but let's be honest— nobody's invented a new move in the last two hundred years. So, although I always give it my all when playing a sport, I have long realized my efforts at tennis are, sadly, extremely unlikely ever to bring me recognition for an original move.

* * *

While the TV broadcasts an Olympic gymnastics competition, Daddy serves—but he cheats, hitting the ball while I watch Simone do her floor exercise. It bounces high over my head, and he scores an ace for 15-0. Some people call it "15-love," but there's not much love on this side of the living room today.

Clearly, with my altitude disadvantage, I need Simone's jumping abilities. This time, I'm ready. As Daddy winds up for his next serve, I launch into a roundoff, back handspring, and a flip in the pike position. My height is perfect, but my timing? Not so much. I miscalculate, do a spectacular face plant, and end up with my rear legs high overhead.

But wait! My back left paw deflects the ball mid-tumble, sending it soaring. In a flash, I'm on my feet again, snagging the ball as it falls.

The crowd goes wild. "Ke-ke... Ke-ke... Ke-ke!" they chant.

The judges, however, have dozed off during my historic performance. Will anyone recognize the genius of my new move? Will it be given a name that secures my place in history?

Or will it remain a misunderstood masterpiece—like when I tried to drink from my water bowl while doing a handstand?

But there's no time for that. Keke is down, and the medics spring into action.

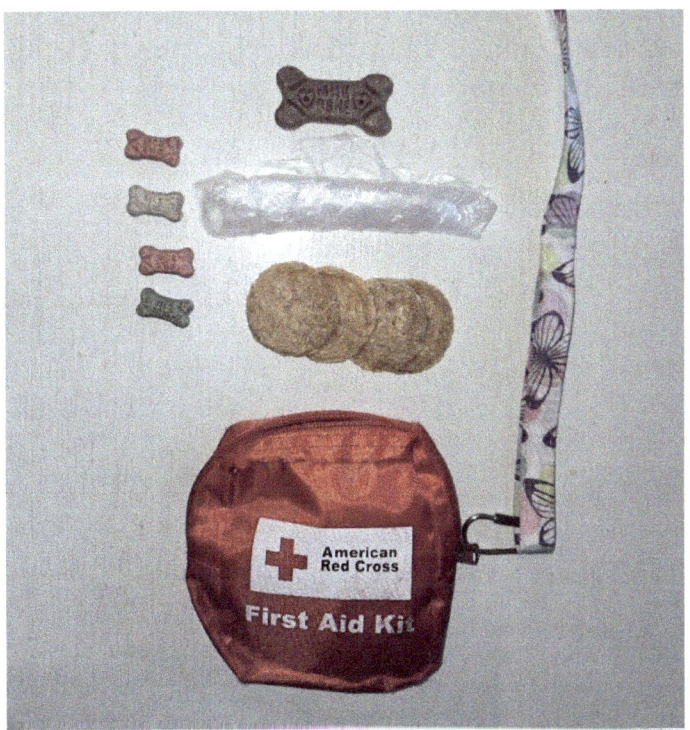

Luckily, Mommy and Daddy always keep a first aid kit attached to my leash. They unclip it, open it up, and carefully spread out the essential medical supplies:

One medium milk-bone dog biscuit

Four small milk-bone dog biscuits

One poop bag

Four chicken chip dog treats

I have to admit, they've thought of everything. I gingerly select a chicken chip—purely for medicinal purposes, of course.

I'm feeling better, but still troubled by the lack of recognition for my groundbreaking move. Since the so-called judges were clearly asleep on the job, it's up to me to name it. I'm thinking something like the "Keke Double-Paw Spinning Flip of Glory" or maybe the "Keke Triple Twirl with a Sassy Finish."

Finally, the Mommy judge speaks.

"Let's call that *Buns Over Teacup*."

Hmmm. Maybe she *was* watching after all.

Pawprints in the Concrete

Nothing boosts morale like a good nap

It was a lazy Sunday afternoon, and Daddy and I rocked gently in our hammock. He snored like a malfunctioning leaf blower, and I basked in the warmth of the sun, watching wispy clouds drift so slowly across the sky that if you blinked, nothing happened. Even the dragonflies, usually zipping around like caffeinated acrobats, had called it quits, lounging on the hydrangea bushes like tiny, winged retirees.

I don't know when Daddy woke up, but I heard him sigh and looked over to find him staring at the clouds too.

"Did you know the Romans invented the siesta?" he mused.

I did not, but I also wasn't sure he was talking to me. Humans often like to blurt out random thoughts into the void, and at times like these, I pride myself on being an excellent listener. I gave him an encouraging ear twitch.

"The word comes from the Latin *sexta*, meaning 'the sixth hour.' Back then, people started work early, so it was time for a nap by mid-afternoon."

A civilization built on mandated nap time? Now *that* was an advanced society.

"Ever wonder how they built mighty empires if everyone took a break in the afternoon?"

I had not. But now I did.

"I can imagine the scene now." He cleared his throat and raised his 'serious historical reenactment' voice.

"Governor Varus: *Primus! Get the Centurions in formation! We march to the Rhine today to crush those puny Germans at dawn!"*

Now his voice shifted to a cockney accent—why a Brit was in Ancient Rome, I had no idea. It was probably the only accent he could do.

"**Primus Pilus:** *Sorry, Guv, the Centurions are nappin'.*

Varus: *They're WHAT?!*

Pilus: *You know how cranky they get without their sexta. Last time we tried skipping it, half the army quit and opened a vineyard!*

Varus: *But we're preparing for battle!*

Pilus: *Sorry, mate—union rules.*"

Daddy sighed and shook his head. "Naps are so misunderstood. The Romans knew that resting during the hottest part of the day saved them from heat stroke, and also meant workers came back refreshed and ready to be productive again. And with the help of the sexta, they built aqueducts—miles of engineering brilliance that let water flow into cities for drinking, bathing, and splashing in puddles."

Puddles! I wagged. Now he was speaking my language.

"And let's not forget concrete! That magical goop that lets humans build sturdy structures that last forever."

Forever, I thought? Or at least until cracks appear, making perfect hidey holes for baby geckos. And more importantly, what better way to leave a legacy than by prancing through freshly poured pavement?

Maximus, go fetch my blankey!

The best way to enjoy a summer siesta is to stretch out under a shady tree with your best friend. Maybe you have a hammock, maybe you're nestled in the grass, or maybe you're sprawled on the couch, belly up, in an air-conditioned lanai.

Honestly, the *where* matters far less than the *who*.

Who is warm and snuggly? Who doesn't snore like a clogged vacuum? Who will wipe the concrete off my paws after I've immortalized myself in history?

Daddy? Meh.

Mommy? Hmmm.

Decisions, decisions.

Another kind of nap

I just returned from a trip to the doctor. This was NOT one of the naps I was looking forward to!

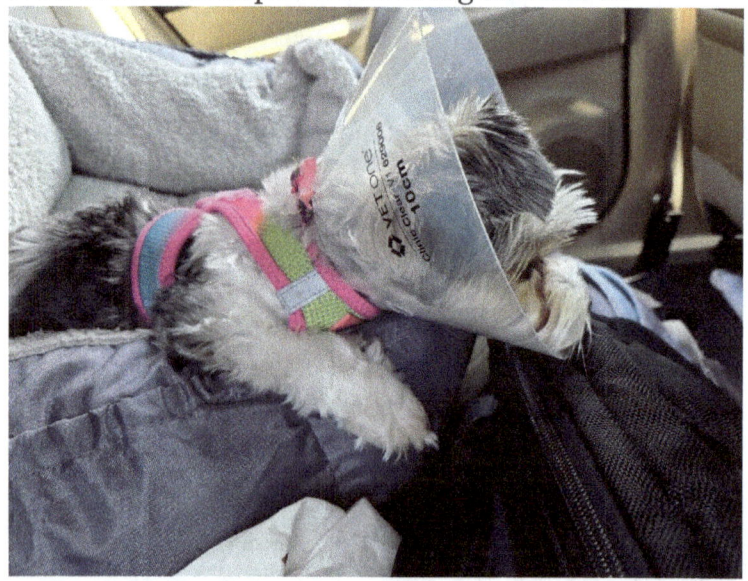

To be continued...

Broken? But You Said I Was Perfect!

You are not a misfit, and you don't need fixing

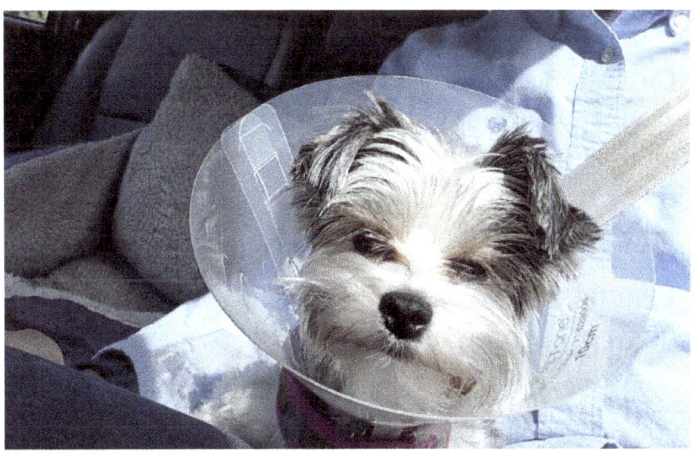

This week, Mommy and Daddy took me to a place called the "Misfit Low-Cost Spay/Neuter Clinic." Misfit? Excuse me, but I am the definition of perfection. And "low cost"? I'm priceless!

But Daddy drove up, waited his turn in a line of cars, and then handed me out the car window like a deposit at the bank. And I didn't even get to take the fun ride up the vacuum tube!

The "teller" who received me had black hair and a face so green and scrunched it looked like she'd just chewed a lemon. Before I could bark a protest, she plopped me into a cage to "wait my turn."

My turn for what? Belly rubs? Treats? A starring role in a movie? I don't think so.

We entered a small room stacked with cages, like a jailhouse for pets. Each cell was occupied—six dogs and three cats, all in solitary confinement, sharing their tales of woe. A Basset Hound crooned a blues number so soulful it could've been recorded in Memphis. A black cat lay curled in the corner, its tail flicking against the bars like an ominous metronome, punctuating its chilling mews of terror.

Could their stories be true? Was this the place where bad puppies and naughty kitties who missed the litter box were sent? Did the evil doctors really "fix" you so you'd never pee or poop again? My tail tucked just thinking about it.

I launched into my own spiritual, a heartfelt rendition promising to improve my "accident-free service record" if I could just be spared. "I'll make Mommy and Daddy proud!" I yowled. "I'll never bark during nap time again!"

But my aria fell on deaf ears. The others were too busy rehearsing their own operas of despair.

After what felt like centuries in my dusty, cobwebbed prison cell, a young, blonde-haired woman appeared. "Okay, Keke, you're next!" she chirped in a high-pitched, sing-song voice. She reminded me of Glinda, the Good Witch. If I had to be snatched away by a witch, at least it was the good one, right?

My mind drifted to ruby slippers and clicking my paws together to get home. Maybe this was all just a dream? But then—WHAM! A sharp pain stabbed my delicate hindquarters. I yelped in betrayal, my eyes wide as saucers.

As the room swirled around me and my legs buckled, I heard Glinda whisper sweetly, "Nap time,

Keke…" Her smile was the last thing I saw before darkness claimed me.

* * *

A black-haired monkey perched in an enormous tree, his wings flapping lazily as he rocked back and forth, chattering nonsense. Beside him, a large gray squirrel sat nibbling on an acorn. To my utter shock, I realized I was tied to a neighboring branch, trussed up like a holiday ham.

The squirrel paused mid-chew and turned to me. "Keke," it said in a familiar, high-pitched voice, "time to go home."

I blinked in disbelief. "Go home?" I yelped, struggling against my bonds. Just then, a pair of hands swooped me off the branch, and a sharp sting pierced my belly.

"Ow!" I barked, twisting to look at my abductor.

The squirrel's voice rang out again. "I'm so sorry, Keke! Did I catch your stitches?"

I opened my eyes and saw it wasn't a squirrel at all but Glinda, carrying me to the door. I tried to turn my head, but something stopped me. It was like I had my own personal fishbowl stuck to my face. A curved, see-through wall extended past my nose, stubbornly following my every move.

Then I remembered Fozzie warning me about the dreaded cone.

"It's like falling down a well, except the well follows you everywhere."

When he got "fixed," they stuck one of these contraptions on his head.

"It's the worst," he said. "Every time you try to sniff the ground—bam! The cone hits first, and you look like a total doofus."

I thought maybe I understood. This was the punishment for bad puppies who pee or poop in the house—they're considered "broken," and while they're being "fixed," they're sent to the cone zone. But something still felt... off. Besides gaining a fishbowl, I couldn't shake the feeling that I'd lost something. Like I'd been robbed of a friend, but I wasn't quite sure who.

Outside, Mommy stood waiting, her face lighting up when she saw me. I tried to give her a slurp of affection, but as soon as I stretched, the pain in my belly hit me like a squeaky toy to the snout. I yelped in protest.

"Oh, Keke, just sit still," Mommy said softly. "Let me take you from the doctor."

With great care, Glinda handed me over—with my ridiculous head-window—to Mommy. I felt like fragile cargo being transferred from one ship to another. Mommy carried me to the car, where Daddy was waiting, holding a small cup of water like it was the Holy Grail.

"Here you go, sweetie," Daddy said, angling the cup toward my snout. I tried to sip, but the cone caught the rim with a resounding clunk. Daddy adjusted, finding the right angle, and I managed a few precious drops before he clicked me into my harness.

As the car hummed to life, I sank into the seat with a groan. We were finally headed home.

* * *

The next day, I felt better. My cone was gone, and I was ready to play. Determined, I dug my tennis ball out of the toy basket and pranced over to Daddy. I dropped it at his feet and gave him my best *this-is-your-purpose-in-life* look.

He sighed, picked up the ball, and gave it the laziest push ever. It rolled about three feet before stopping, wobbling sadly like a deflated balloon.

What kind of game is this, Daddy? C'mon, put some muscle into it! I need airtime!

But instead of throwing it properly, Daddy set the ball aside and gave me a serious look. His shoulders slumped, and he smelled... sad.

"I'm sorry, Keke," he said gently. "I need to tell you a couple of things."

I plopped down next to him to wait for the bad news. Was he going to tell me we were out of treats? Or, worse, that the Blue Jays had taken over the backyard?

"The doctor says you need to rest for two weeks because of your surgery," Daddy continued. "We can't play fetch for a while."

I looked at him. He looked back at me, then continued.

"And you should understand what's going on," he said. "Because you're such a small dog, it would be dangerous for you to have puppies. That's why you had to get fixed. I'm afraid you'll never be able to have puppies of your own."

I stared at him, horrified, as the truth sank in.

Wait... what did you just say?! No playtime? TWO WHOLE WEEKS?!

That's like fourteen years in dog time! How can I possibly survive without running, jumping, or tugging toys? No zoomies? No squirrel-chasing?

OMG, this is officially the WORST DAY of my life EVER!

The Phone Ate My Human's Brain

Can your human remove the lid from a dog food can when YouTube is down?

If there's one thing humans love more than dogs, it's their phones.

Sad, but true. They carry those shiny rectangles everywhere, staring at them like they hold the secrets of the universe—or at least the location of the nearest kale juice stand. They use them to organize their love lives, track their steps, and check their vitals. It's like they're treating themselves like dogs, except the phones don't even spit out treats. And trust me, kale juice is not a treat.

Wrong reasons to use smartphones

I believe there are appropriate times and places for humans to use phones, and there are unsuitable ones— am I right? We all need to keep our wits (and senses) about us when walking because we never know when the next car will whiz by, the sidewalk will be caked with trodden poop, or the neighbor's cat will send a gecko flying for its life. You don't want to miss any of them, do you?

The list of *wrong* reasons to use phones is too extensive, so it's easier to enumerate the...

Right reasons to use smartphones

Here are some acceptable applications:

1. Take a photogenic picture of their favorite dog. Because who doesn't need twenty-five photos of their dog every day?

2. Sending texts to other dog lovers. To let other humans know how great we are, or send the aforementioned photos.

3. Plan the route to the nearest pet store. To ensure the quickest path to get more dog treats, of course.

4. Watching dog videos. Humans like watching videos of other dogs, probably just to see how much more fun their own dogs are.

5. Play a fun dog-focused game, such as "Bark Park!" (a multiplayer game to become the king tinkler).

Some people say phone apps can help them manage their money. I'm not sure why they're so focused on these worthless green chew toys, but if it gets more gifts for their favorite dog, I'm all for it.

They can also use their phone to call ahead for reservations at their favorite dog-friendly restaurant. Here's a sign I saw at The Tavares Dog House, a restaurant that has a large outdoor seating area:

Imperfect tool or unbelievable nuisance?

And then there are those constant 'ding!' and 'buzz!' sounds that come from their phones all day long. Humans react every time, like someone rang a bell and promised them a treat. Only instead of a tasty snack, it's just another boring email. Meanwhile, I'm sitting right there, looking cute, waiting for them to throw the ball— or better yet, the bacon.

And for what? Half the time, it's something useless like, 'Your package is three stops away!' (Translation: Not here yet—*keep obsessing.*) Or 'Don't forget to drink water!' (*Seriously? You need an app for that?*) And then there's 'This Day in History!'—because apparently, what happened in the Stone Age is more important than the fact that I'm standing right here with my squeaky Lamb Chop, waiting for a game of tug-of-war.

Dogs have chew toys; humans have '*you toys*'— because every time you stare into that screen, it's all about you. Come on, man! Priorities!

Withdrawals

As with any junkie, your humans will be devastated if they lose their phone or if an essential service is down.

Try to be understanding when they start muttering under their breath, "TikTok, tick tock, how long has it been out?" Or wandering the streets aimlessly without a GPS signal. Or going to a party with nothing to say because their favorite A.I. chatbot can't write any zingers and TMZ is down.

Does your human assume the fetal position and cry like a baby when they've misplaced their phone? Do they need help removing the lid from a dog food can because YouTube is not responding?

Take a deep breath, dear human. Look down—see me? Tail wagging, eyes full of love, ready for a cuddle or a game of fetch? That's your real notification. And trust me, it's way more important than whatever just buzzed in your pocket.

Now, how about we go outside? No apps required.

Happy National Puppy Day

Make sure they honor you on your special day!

March 23 is National Puppy Day. Finally, a holiday that celebrates the most important creatures on Earth—puppies! (Me!) Today is your chance to honor the joy, wisdom, and boundless energy that we bring into your life. And what better way to celebrate than by learning a little more about yours truly?

You see, I may be small, but I've lived a stupendously large life. And I've thrived while experiencing incredible changes since coming into this world. Let's look at some of the changes.

Exit through the gift shop—NOT!

The biggest change in my life happened on April 20, 2023. The morning started like any other: dark, slobbery, and crowded. I mean crammed. We're talking nose-to-privates, get-your-tongue-out-of-my-ear levels of congestion. Life had always been this way—at least, for as long as I could remember—but lately, my home was getting as overcrowded as Nick's Tavern during Happy Hour on paycheck day. (Not that I would know anything about that firsthand. Just something I've, uh, heard.)

But that day, things started moving. The noses, the paws, the tails—even the walls started shifting like we were trapped in a living, breathing, furry roller coaster. Then, without warning, I was being squeezed, sloshed, and turned in every direction at once, like a sock in a washing machine. (*Oh! The washing machine story! But I'll save that one for another day.*)

Just when I thought I couldn't take any more, a mysterious opening appeared. It was small, but bright, and it pulsed like it couldn't decide whether it wanted to be open or closed. Then someone behind me started pushing, shouting, "Your turn! Your turn!" There may have also been some bad words I'm not allowed to repeat.

And then—POP!—I was shoved out into the cold, bright world like a drunk getting booted from Nick's. (Again, just something I've heard about. Never happened to me personally. Honest.)

And what was waiting for me at the end of this wild ride? A gift shop? Nope. Just more slobber, a lot of noise, and—*worst of all*—the realization that my unlimited buffet had been replaced by a first-come, first-served, every-pup-for-themselves scramble. What kind of exit strategy is that?

I was born with two brothers and a sister, and let me tell you—there was chaos. There was competition. There were complaints to management. And I'm pretty sure Momma didn't really mean all those bad names she called us.

No returns, no exchanges

The next big event happened on the last day of June when I adopted my new humans and then promptly took control of their house. I had it spruced up and smelling like a proper kennel in no time, then received my diploma at house training graduation.

(For details, see my lesson, "Part 1 of House Training for Puppies: A Little Dab'll Do Ya," from my earlier book, *The Dog Park Massacre*.)

There were many lessons to teach my humans, who were new to this puppy-parenting business. For instance, they needed to learn to keep their paws off my blog, the secrets of a stress-free road trip (it's more fun for everyone if someone rides in the back with me), and how to lead happier, longer lives (*spoiler alert: eat like a dog*).

So, let's celebrate the wonders that we live with on National Puppy Day!

If you're a puppy, I hope your humans take this opportunity to shower you with gifts and special favors—like a squeaky toy so annoying that the neighbors three doors down will appreciate your joy. Or a giant bone bigger than your head (but you'll spend the next hour trying to figure out how to get it off the couch).

If you're a human, I hope you have a puppy to play with today. If not, visit an animal shelter and find her. *Hurry, she's waiting for you!*

How to Keep Your Human in Shape

(Before They Need Wheels and a Ramp)

Humans love their "New Year's resolutions." Every January, they solemnly vow to "get in shape," then celebrate their progress by binge-watching *Grey's Anatomy* from the couch while fork-lifting nachos shaped like dumbbells. Fitness clubs draw new members faster than squirrels raiding a bird feeder, only to watch most humans vanish by February—like cats when it's time to visit the vet.

Forget the "quick fix" solutions. That's where we dogs come in. As "man's best friend," we don't just love and protect our humans—we also invigorate them and keep them moving. We attack this responsibility with the intensity of a Chihuahua in a squeaky toy aisle.

And let's face it. Humans without canine supervision are disasters waiting to happen. They get heart disease, they stress-eat entire pepperoni pizzas, and they sit motionless for hours glued to reruns on *Netflix*. I shudder to think of those poor, dogless souls wandering through life like lost mail carriers.

Luckily, I have a foolproof plan. I consume leftovers, calm my people down when they're overtaxed, design a daily exercise regimen, and provide a friendly reminder service to keep them on track. I help my humans in all the ways they never knew they needed. Sure, they didn't *ask* me to take over, but waiting for human input is like waiting for them to stop scrolling Facebook: they'd be wheeling down the halls of the nursing home singing "Copacabana" in their tricked-out custom-made wheelchair before we even got started.

Basic exercise: the walk

There are many ways to exercise, so we'll start with the basics. I begin with thrice-daily walks. Walking increases cardiovascular fitness, strengthens bones, and improves your chances of a successful getaway when Auntie Mildred comes to visit.

Once our walk starts, I take breaks when my human gets fatigued by providing opportunities for sniffing, greeting neighbors, and stretching. Bending to scoop the daily missile improves flexibility and balance and provides a pleasing cologne when meeting new neighbors.

Scooping poop also improves fine motor skills. Have you ever tried to open a plastic poop bag? It's like convincing a peacock to tone down its feather display.

More advanced exercise

Once your human gets on a daily walking schedule, it's time to take the workout to the next level. I keep the emphasis on fun, and the most popular outdoor exercise for dog-loving humans is one they call "fetch."

The game usually involves your human throwing an object—anything from a stick to a space-age glider—for us to retrieve. The trouble is that humans have found creative ways to put the entire exercise burden on the dog.

First, it's in their choice of projectile. A tennis ball is the favorite, and at first blush, it makes sense. Old tennis balls are in ready supply (often free), have an extended life, and bounce on almost any surface. But I suspect human motivations go beyond these simple advantages.

Second, tennis balls bounce far, which means more running for the dog and less exercise for the human.

Third, inexpensive launchers propel the ball further while humans expend less energy. With these advantages, a human can send a tennis ball hurtling so far that it winds up in orbit around a nearby asteroid.

This sounds very considerate—almost generous—with the human giving their pet more exercise. But consider what the average human does while said dog explores interstellar limits in search of their ball.

You know what I'm referring to already, don't you? While the dog searches nearby nebulae, the human explores the netherworlds of Instagram on their phone. Yes, these exercises are very one-sided, and as "man's best friend," it's your job to even the game and extend the workout to multiple body parts. A heavily exercised scrolling finger does not a fit human make.

If you're a big bruiser of a dog like my Labrador friend Logan, you can chew the tennis ball until it won't bounce anymore. If your human continues using it, at least you've reduced the carry distance and shortened the smartphone break.

If you're a smaller dog like me, taking the edge off a tennis ball's bounce may require long periods of chafing, like an athlete who wears the same jockstrap every day for three years. Keep at it. If you ever need to clamp down on a wayward hot dog or, heaven forbid, Uncle Dave's gym shorts, you'll be glad you had the practice.

Set boundaries

Consider the escalation that usually accompanies the game of "fetch." Your human starts with short throws because, as cheap as used tennis balls may be, humans are cheaper, and they don't want to lose the ball. In addition to thrift, they initially throw short to ensure the dog understands the game and builds the stamina for interplanetary travel. They gradually increase the throw until the integrity of the tennis ball is threatened by an impending core-collapse supernova.

As a dog, you need to do two things: <u>set some boundaries</u> and be *in*consistent. Keep the throw within the same solar system and keep them guessing whether you will return it. Now and then, pretend you didn't see the throw and make that two-footed high-stepping all-that punker fetch his own ball. Act like a cat: aloof, unpredictable, and just smug enough to make them question their choices.

And remember, if all else fails, just take the ball and run. The heart rate spike from sheer panic when they think they've lost it will do wonders for their cardiovascular health.

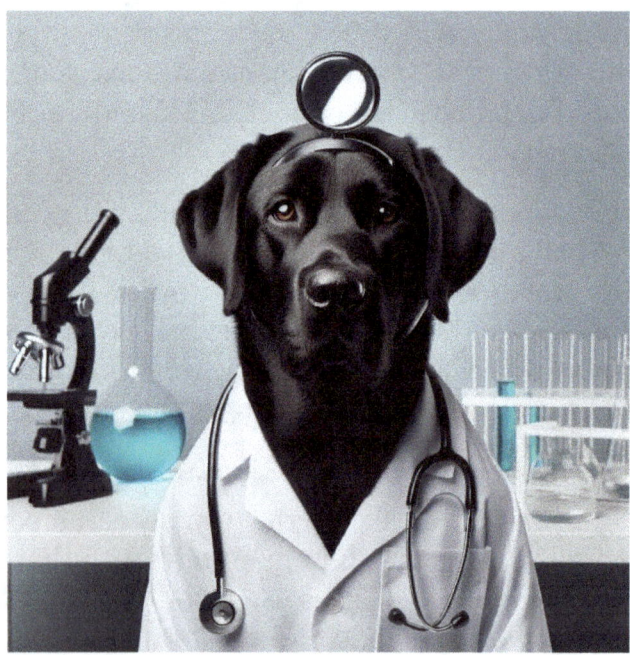

Note: This story is not a substitute for professional medical advice. If in doubt, consult my Labrador friend Logan. His *lab tests* are guaranteed.

Finding Your Dream Job

Ten suggestions for finding that new vocation that's perfect for you

Okay, so the home security gig is getting old, and you're feeling unappreciated. Like last week, when Daddy yelled at me—*really yelled*—when I tried to sound the intruder alert.

"Keke, hush!"

Was it my fault the neighbor's lawnmower backfired with a force that would make a thunderclap sound like a polite tap on the door?

What choice do I have if a van driving by makes that same "chunka-chunka-chunk" sound the U.P.S. truck makes?

Let's face it: many humans fail to cherish their live-in home security systems enough. Nor do they reward us adequately. I can identify two-thirds of our home visitors by the sound of their footfalls—a far better rate than a Ring doorbell—yet I'm working for Pupperonis that can be picked up at the grocery store for $4.99 a bag. And I don't even get a whole stick after successfully shaking down the UPS guy.

Speaking of shake-downs, look at my record. On one day alone last week, I raided the Amazon truck and brought home a Taylor Swift 1989 CD (Taylor's version), an iPhone screen protector two-pack, and a Harry & David gift basket with seventy-five percent of the contents intact.

Who else can give that rate of return? Yet Daddy focused solely on the missing twenty-five percent. Talk about tunnel vision!

If you're like me, you may be considering new opportunities or a second job. One that will be rewarding and exciting—or perhaps won't require hazard pay. One that will increase your self-esteem and help break you out of that rut. Or at least yield some better treats.

Ten new job opportunities to consider

Here, I present ten job possibilities for the underappreciated canine.

1. Hairstylist

You'll be a natural at cutting shag styles, but this might not be the best headshot for your business card:

2. Food deliverer

These jobs are highly desirable because of the perks, but hard to find. Some previous couriers gave us a bad reputation for partial deliveries.

3. Dishwasher

You are so much more than just a pre-wash cycle.

4. French chef

Dogs would make excellent French chefs—after all, we have an innate appreciation for rich, meaty flavors, and no one savors duck liver quite like we do.

Step one: teach the Foie Gras to come when called.

5. Interior decorator

Dogs have a keen eye for space optimization—just look at how efficiently we rearrange couch cushions, blankets, and even freshly folded laundry into the perfect nest. We also excel at texture selection, preferring only the finest, most chewable materials.

Of course, your clients might not realize you're colorblind and wonder why you keep referring to the blue wall.

6. Mail Carrier

Dogs have an unparalleled sense of direction—just try getting lost on a walk when you've taken the same route twice. Our speed and enthusiasm ensure prompt deliveries, and we take the security of every package very seriously (even if we occasionally inspect them with our teeth).

But resist the urge to chase your co-workers.

7. Teacher

Dogs make natural teachers—we're patient, persistent, and excellent at positive reinforcement (just try ignoring us when we want a back scratch). We also believe in paws-on learning—because the best way to understand something is to chew on it for a while.

However, claims that the teacher ate your homework may not be received well.

8. Taste tester

Dogs make excellent gourmet samplers—we have an unrivaled enthusiasm for sampling anything remotely edible (and some things that aren't). Somebody needs to ensure the use of only quality ingredients. But take it easy on the nitrates, please!

9. Lap dancer

Some jobs require years of training, but some things you're just a natural at! Lap dancing? Nailed it.

10.   Friend

But the most fulfilling job may be "man's best friend." Even when nobody else wants to be around him. Even when he yells at you for no good reason. Because sometimes, the best job in the world isn't the one with the best perks—it's the one that matters most.

And sometimes we all just need someone we can count on, don't we?

Understanding Human Packs

Bonding Lessons from a four-legged alien

Sometimes, I feel like Harry Vanderspeigle, the extraterrestrial who crash-lands on Earth in *Resident Alien* and gradually learns the secrets of humanity. Humans are tough nuts to crack, and like Harry, I spend a good deal of time wondering about these peculiar beings I've taken up with. What drives their pack? Why do they love or hate certain humans? Or dogs, for that matter?

Humans bond for the strangest reasons. Sometimes, it's proximity and a desire to protect one another. I get that. There's strength in numbers, so my ancestors, the wolves, traveled in packs.

We may be able to learn more about human behavior by comparing their packs to ours:

1. Pack Hierarchy

In a wolf pack, the alpha leads the group with authority and strength. In a human pack, the alpha is often the one holding the remote control or the car keys, but their leadership can be overridden by whoever shouts, "I don't care, you pick!" the loudest.

2. Hunting Tactics

Wolves run together for miles to track and take down prey. Humans, on the other hand, hunt solo by swiping through delivery apps. The closest thing to a coordinated hunt is arguing over which pizza toppings to order. It may also be interesting to compare hunting tactics to those of cats. Male lions, for instance, send the lionesses to do all the work while they nap in the shade. Typical of every house cat I've seen (and many male humans, come to think of it).

3. Marking Territory

Wolves use scent to define their range. Humans use "No Soliciting" signs, garden gnomes, or Wi-Fi networks with names like "GetOffMyLawn."

4. Pack Bonding

Wolves bond by playing, grooming, and sharing meals. Humans bond by sitting silently in a room, each staring at their own glowing rectangle.

5. Howling

Wolves howl to communicate over long distances. Humans shout into their phones, or worse, make bizarre howling noises when singing karaoke.

6. Conflict Resolution

Wolves settle disputes with posturing and occasional nips. Humans engage in prolonged passive-aggressive battles, like leaving the toilet seat up or "forgetting" whose turn it is to do the dishes.

7. Raising Pups

In a wolf pack, everyone pitches in to raise the young. In a human pack, raising pups often involves handing them a tablet and praying they don't start throwing things during dinner.

Other packs

Humans can belong to more than one pack, which opens up a world of gratuitous benefits for them. A single human can herd with one group that loves Dachshunds, another that hunts for the latest Groupon bargains, and still another that hangs out at the dog park to get the newest gossip.

Appearances

Some humans unite over skin or hair color. Others think they're prettier than everyone else and refuse to gather with people who fail to meet their standards. I get the attraction—everyone flocks to me because I'm the cutest puppy on the block. But hey, I could even share a burger with a Shar Pei.

But a cat? Well... even *I* have standards.

Like Harry Vanderspeigle, I recognize the diversity of the universe and the absurdity of human preferences. But it doesn't take an alien to alienate. Just remember: labels don't define you.

We can all shake our labels. But only dogs can shake their tails.

The Bird Poop Chronicles (Part 1)

It's a fine mess you've gotten yourself into this time, Keke

It all started on my daily walks with Daddy, and it was innocent enough in the beginning. Spring was in the air, and so were the Blue Jays, Cardinals, and Goldfinches. Everywhere, there was the scent of fresh flowers and equally fresh squirrels, chasing each other in an exciting game of "tail tag."

It inspired me to play some games of my own. Daddy's hold on the leash kept my choice of partners to a minimum, but sometimes it's fun even to play games with him.

Catch Me If You Can: Bird Poop Edition

Ah, bird poop: the forbidden snack. The delicacy no one talks about but every dog relishes. The objective of the game is simple: Spot a pile of bird poop and gobble it before Daddy has a chance to pull the leash and say, "No, Keke!"

Daddy can be surprisingly fast on the leash sometimes, but I'm faster and more determined.

We were walking through the neighborhood one morning when I spotted a small black-and-white pile of bird poop glistening in the sunlight like a dog food condiment. Daddy was, as usual, absorbed in his phone, so I capitalized on the opportunity and darted toward the poop, my snout and tongue in ready anticipation.

"Keke, no!" Daddy shouted, but it was too late. Keke one, Daddy zero.

He muttered something about "disgusting habits," but I ignored him. Humans just don't understand the thrill of the game.

That evening, though, things took a turn. And so did my stomach. The rumbles grew louder and angrier, and before long, I was dashing for the front yard like a Golden Retriever in pursuit of his *Chuckit* Flying Squirrel. But let me tell you, it was less like a fun game of *Fetch* and more like a game of *Retch*.

By the time Daddy caught up to me, I was hunched over in a very unladylike position, looking as guilty as a dog caught chewing a new pair of shoes. "Oh, Keke..." he said, his voice a mix of sympathy and exasperation.

And the next thing I knew, I was in the car headed for my least favorite place in the world: the vet's office. Now, don't get me wrong. Dr. Gallo is nice enough, but there are places thermometers should never go.

Daddy explained the situation to Dr. Gallo while I gave him my best "pitiful puppy look." He nodded knowingly, like this happened every day. It turns out I'm not the only dog who's fallen victim to the bird poop's siren song.

Pill spitting

The vet prescribed a little pill, which we brought home.

I've been taking lessons from Zoey, the family cat, on "politely declining" pills. Usually, I do my best to avoid doing anything a cat suggests, but I have to admit they know how to take a pill with style. Or not take it, as the case may be.

When we got home, Daddy tried recreating the vet's smooth technique. He held the pill in one hand and a glob of peanut butter in the other. I played along at first, opening my mouth when he asked nicely. But as soon as the pill hit my tongue, I spat it out with the precision of a catapult, sending it flying across the kitchen. Daddy sighed, picked it up, and tried again. This time, he buried it deeper in the peanut butter, which I licked off like the gourmet connoisseur I am, and—plop!—out came the pill.

By round three, Daddy tried hiding it in a piece of chicken. Nice try, but I chewed carefully, eating around the pill like a surgeon performing a delicate operation.

Daddy groaned. "Keke, you're impossible."

I wagged my tail. Keke four, Daddy zero.

By the next day, Daddy was using cheese instead of peanut butter. Now, cheese is a rare treat, normally reserved for special occasions or when Daddy feels guilty about something. He held the pill out triumphantly, wrapped in a gooey cube of cheddar, and said, "Here you go, Keke. Your favorite!"

I sniffed it, wagging my tail to lull him into a false sense of security. Then, in one smooth move, I snatched the cheese, swallowed it, and spat the pill onto the floor before he could blink.

Daddy stared at me in disbelief. "Seriously?!"

Bullseye! Or... not

When the urgency of my poop delivery reached critical levels, Mommy and Daddy put down pee-pee pads for me. I hadn't used these in many months, so I appreciated it when Mommy gave me a refresher course.

"Here, Keke," Mommy said, clapping her hands. "Do your business *here*." I wanted her to demonstrate, but she pretended not to understand.

The game was like dart-throwing. I was never any good at hitting a bullseye with a dart, and I'm no better with poop. I sniffed the pad, circled it, and settled on what seemed like the perfect spot. Humans can be so critical, as I observed in Daddy's response. "She's not even close!"

Honestly, I tried, but runnies fall as runnies doo.

I treated it like a game of darts, and the next attempt was closer—a solid edge hit. Mommy gave me a half-hearted "Good try, Keke," while Daddy cleaned up the mess with a sigh.

Catch me if you can: Butt-wiping edition

Just when I thought humans couldn't get more ridiculous, they decided my butt needed special attention.

"Keke, come here," Mommy said, armed with a wet wipe. She crouched down, all sweet and smiley, like I didn't know what she was planning.

But I knew.

And so, the chase began. I darted under the coffee table, zoomed around the couch, and slid across the kitchen floor like Enzo, the race car dog from *The Art of Racing in the Rain*.

When they finally cornered me, Daddy held me while Mommy cleaned me up with a wipe.

Thanks to canine physiology, we're quite capable of taking care of this all by ourselves, thank you very much!

Two on one, with four opposable thumbs: the only way they can catch me!

As my friend Kanga, the English Bulldog, would say, "Bloody amateurs."

* * *

By the end of the week, my appetite was gone, and I was exhausted. That's when they packed me up and put me in the car. This time, an unknown man in a lab coat greeted me. His demeanor was as gentle as his thermometer, and his humor as warm as his stethoscope. A doctor, no doubt.

"We're going to play a game," the doctor said.

Oh, no, I've had enough of games.

"This one's called, 'behave so I can fix you up.'"

That sounded like a one-sided game if there was one. *I bet your girlfriend doesn't rush to the door to greet you when you come home, does she?*

I was doing my best to monitor all his hands—I swear there were more than two—when I felt a sharp sting like a fire ant in my back left leg. I turned to face my attacker and discovered the kind, smiling face of a woman.

"I'm sorry, Keke," she said. "I hope that didn't hurt too much, but we need to start an I.V."

While I was pondering her words, the woman wrapped tape around my leg and attached a tube to a bag. As I watched, I felt dizzy and found my eyelids growing heavy.

I heard Mommy say, "It's okay, Keke. Just take a little nap." And I found a familiar-smelling blanket beneath me as I curled up.

To be continued...

The Bird Poop Chronicles (Conclusion)

In dog we trust

I dreamed I was playing soccer with a bunch of porcupines, but the prickly little potatoes kept popping the balls and running them across the goal line. I said that's okay. I understood they didn't mean to pop the balls, but their goals couldn't count if the ball was flat. I reminded them of "Deflate-gate." They bristled and started shooting quills at me. I ducked, but one hit me in the back leg and another in my behind. I tried to run away, but they had me surrounded.

I woke with a yelp, shivering and biting at my leg. I huddled on my blanket in a cold, unfamiliar cage. The bright room smelled of disinfectant. A small black kitten mewed in a cage to my left, and a French Poodle yapped to my right. I speak little French, but his barks rendered fear and loneliness. For once, I had to agree with a poodle.

I didn't know where I was or who these strange animals were. Would they try to hurt me? Where were Mommy and Daddy when I needed them?

The nurse from earlier entered the room and opened my cage.

"Keke, you're awake," she said with a smile. "Let's see how you're doing."

Oh, no. I know what that means—poking and probing on a cold steel table, sticking innocent puppies with needles. No, thanks.

Usually, I can squirm out of human hands quicker than a squirrel can raid a nut store on Black Friday. Unfortunately, I wasn't myself. The last time I checked, I was a pincushion waiting for a team of seamstresses.

The head seamstress carried me into a room and handed me to Mommy. I was so happy to see her that I got my energy back and immediately climbed up Mommy's chest to shower her with slobbery love droplets.

"My sweet baby," Mommy said, trying to speak between puppy licks. "You poor thing. Don't phwath pith blah—*yuck!*"

It felt good to hear her reassuring voice, even if she made no sense.

"Hold still," she said, "and be good for the doctor."

Wait! Don't let him take me again!

Mommy held me while the doctor poked and prodded.

Finally, Mommy looked me in the eye and said, "Keke, you need to hear what the doctor has to say."

He eyed me, then spoke in stern words punctuated with a finger that tapped me on the forehead in emphasis. "You need to stop eating things outside, Keke. You got sick and runny from eating bird poop. And you need to take your medicine, or you won't get better, and you'll be back here again." He raised an eyebrow. "Understand?"

I gulped, my ears drooping.

We drove home in silence, then Daddy took me for a walk.

It felt like weeks since I'd been here. The sun warmed my coat, the birds sang happy tunes, and I watched in awe as a squirrel jumped from tree to tree above our heads.

I sniffed and found a little nugget on the ground. It had the wondrous odor of day-old Cardinal poop. The Cardinals in our neighborhood seemed to eat like royalty. Their poop smelled of fresh fruits, even in the wintertime, and I wondered where they got their food. If I licked it, I might be able to tell.

The tiny nugget was calling, inviting me. What harm would it do to taste it?

I felt the leash tighten. I had paused too long, and Daddy had noticed. I had to work fast to beat him to the punch. "Don't eat it," he warned.

The doctor's voice rang in my ears. "You need to stop eating things outside." What was it he said? The bird poop made me sick?

It was unfair, but I didn't want to get sick again. I lifted my head and kept walking.

Back inside, I walked to my bowl for a drink. I sniffed my dish, and there was the foul-smelling pill. Not broken up. Not mixed with food. Hidden in plain sight.

I had to admire their innovation. But there was something more on that plate. Something much more.

There was honesty. There was trust.

I swallowed the pill and washed it down with a long drink of water.

The Ultimate Alarm Clock

Your children will never wake up in a bad mood again

Do your children have difficulty waking up in the morning? Do you have to remind them five times to get out of bed so they don't miss the bus? Or once they are up, are they drowsy, unproductive, and cranky?

I'm running a limited-time offer: the *Rent-a-Puppy Alarm Clock*. When it's time to get up, simply rub some *KONG Stuff'N Sweet Potato Spread Dog Treat* on your children's faces and then let *Rent-a-Puppy* loose on their beds. Your kids are guaranteed to wake up in an excellent mood. We promise there will be no trace of *Sweet Potato Spread* on their faces when *Rent-a-Puppy* is done, but the smile will last for hours.

Okay, you've accomplished two steps out of three: They're awake, and they're in a good mood. Now, how do you get them out of bed?

Our patented *Barf Alarm* is just the thing, and it's included free with every *Rent-a-Puppy Alarm Clock*. Set the Barf Alarm timer on the puppy's collar before you let her loose. When wake-up time is reached, the collar will emit sounds like a puppy retching, which then escalates to a full-on barf. Your kids will be fighting for the door in no time.

BUT WAIT... there's more!

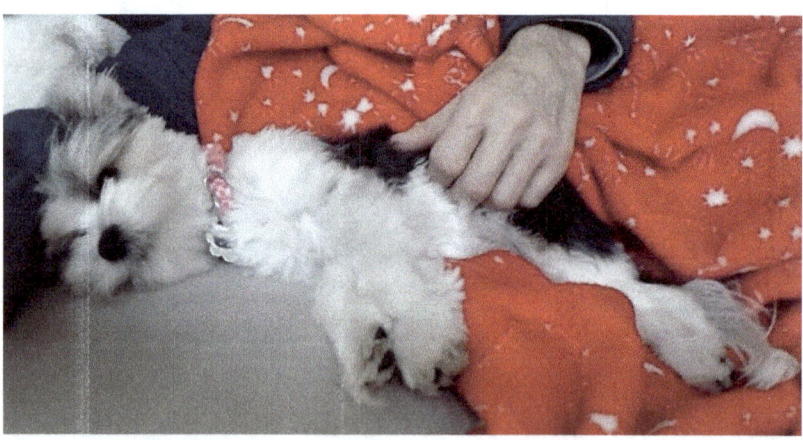

Do your children have difficulty falling asleep at night? Too wound up? Too stressed about exams?

Forget melatonin, yoga, bedtime stories, and boring nights in front of "cool-down" TV programs. How about a warm, soft puppy to lull your insomniac to sleep? For a limited time, you'll receive our patented "Rub-a-Puppy Fuzz Therapy" for free with every *Rent-a-Puppy Alarm Clock*. A proven way to reduce stress, forget worries, and recover from an evening of binge-watching *Stranger Things* on Netflix.

Kid-recommended, puppy-approved

P.S.: Want to own your puppy alarm system? Easy payment plans are available.

"We work for treats!"

Sometimes You Have to Poop in the House

Duties come first

The other day, Daddy and I went for a walk around the neighborhood. When we got home, I used the pee-pee pad in the dining room corner for a quick poop. That's when Daddy lost it.

"Keke," he groaned, pointing at the pad like it was a crime scene. "We were outside for almost thirty minutes. Why did you wait until we got back inside? That pad is for emergencies!"

Emergencies? Clearly, there was a misunderstanding. Couldn't he see how busy I was during our walk? I packed two hours' worth of crucial obligations into that half hour, and he expected me to poop on command?

Maybe it's time I explained just how demanding my workload really is.

From the moment I step outside, smells, sounds, tastes, and sights bombard my senses. Some are familiar, others are foreign. I cannot study them all at once, so I shunt many aside for later investigation.

The first step is a quick inspection to secure the borders. If any intruders are present, they need to be ejected—within the constraints of that blasted leash.

Darn, you silly bipeds! You hire me to do a job and then limit my range, so I can't even reach the limits of the property.

If no current interlopers are detected, I sniff the ground to determine who crossed the lines of demarcation since my last walk. Some are friends, some are foes, and some are just interesting. Did you know 213 earthworms came up for air during the rain last night?

I check friends' scents for health. I note any unidentified intruders for later investigation.

There are sounds everywhere: humans, machines, birds, insects, etc. A constant distraction, even if not relevant to the task at hand.

And the sights! Aside from the squirrels who think they own the place, hawks and buzzards float on the updrafts, yellow Warblers flit from tree to tree, and Cardinals nest in our Oak. Depending on the season, butterflies, bees, and dragonflies crisscross yards and gather around flowers to sip nectar, gossip, or chase each other in little aerial dance routines.

And that's just our yard. Multiply that by thirty or more on a typical walk.

So, forgive me if I'm a little distracted when we go walking. I have bigger fish to fry.

Like the one shown below, which we found on our deck one morning.

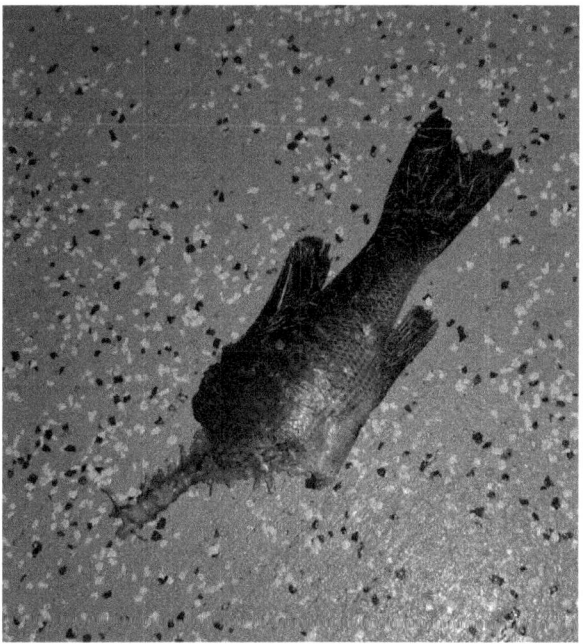

The photo shows the eight-inch-long skeletal remains of a fish—yet the nearest lake is almost a half mile away. I filed this under 'M' for mysteries. Or perhaps that should be for *murder*?

Duties come first. Doodies come later. Isn't that our agreement? Perhaps this little song will help explain it better:

Keke's Busy-ness
(sung to the tune of "I'm Late, I'm Late!")

I'm busy, I'm busy!

No need to have a hissy.

I'm sorry if you're miffed, but I mostly taste and sniff.

I hate debate on stuff they ate

But really must investigate

That's why I took a whiff!

No, no, no, no, no.

No time to pee or poop,

I fortify and snoop,

I track and act and check the facts,

And then I must regroup.

Whoops!

I'm busy, I'm busy!

No need to be a sissy.

So much to chew and sniff and do—

My sample plate is worth the rate

Although you often hesitate—

That's why I'm in a stew!

Whew!

I'm busy, I'm busy! Can't you see I'm busy?

Paradin' o' the Green

A little tomfoolery
that will have you Dublin over with laughter

Sunday was St. Paddy's Day in the U.S., a wonderful holiday commemorating some dude who drove the snakes out of Ireland and replaced them with Guinness breweries. A good trade, most would agree—right up there with getting a second helping of treats before dinner.

It was a day for the wearin' o' the green (and the spray-paintin' o' the green, for some). We came to join the celebrations and march in the parade with our Dynamic Dog Club. I wore shamrocks (because actual rocks were too heavy, arf-arf!).

I was over the rainbow to see Finn, my friendly pup-rechaun. And I wanted to check out the Pomeranian—the cutest clover in the patch—but he rode in a carriage, high above us working-class dogs. I was green with envy.

As our club approached, a boisterous crowd chanted, "Who let the dogs out? Who! Who!"

Who wouldn't? And what's their beef?

People packed the parade route on both sides. I couldn't believe how many came to see me. Who knew green was my color?

Just remember—never iron a four-leaf clover, or you might press your luck!

When the Breeze Turned Bitter

Smelling and tasting a poisoned world

"You know, there are times when it's a source of personal pride to not be human."

-Hobbes (the tiger in Calvin and Hobbes)

Daddy and I were walking in a small city, far enough from home that the smells of our neighborhood were undetectable. Trotting down the sidewalk, I wagged my tail in anticipation of the new sights, sounds, and smells I'd meet on our walk today. Daddy held my leash tightly, guiding me through the urban jungle.

But as we ventured further, my excitement waned. My nose twitched with the acrid scent of exhaust fumes in the morning air.

We turned a corner and entered a park, where I expected solace among the trees, grass, and bushes. Finally, a place more like home!

As we approached a pond, however, it was challenging to find pleasant smells of nature. The water was murky, its surface covered with a filmy scum and floating debris. Discarded bags and other trash clung to the reeds along the shore. Where I was used to hearing birds and seeing ducks by the water's edge, I found beer cans, soda bottles, and small bits of detritus. I reached out to move some debris but recoiled at the foul stench. This was not the refreshing oasis I hoped for.

I was startled by a plastic grocery bag as it swept past me, carried on the breeze, and came to rest in the reeds by the water's edge.

"Plastics are the legacy of humanity," I heard Daddy say. He had a reusable bag in his pocket and stooped to pick up trash, all the while muttering something under his breath about the groundwater and how microplastics make it into the food chain. I continued to watch for signs of life.

It wasn't long before Daddy filled his bag, but my quest for natural scents was unrewarded.

As we left the park and walked along a nearby tree-lined street, I detected the scent of flowers in bloom. I heard the rustle of a small, unseen creature foraging in the leaves under a nearby bush. I stopped to sniff, and although I could not identify its smell, the tiny bit of wildlife I sensed in the polluted city lifted my mood.

As we left the ravages of urban decay, I wondered about its inhabitants. Didn't any nearby residents care enough to pick up the trash left in their park? Did they think it was someone else's job?

Or had they given up hope?

As we returned to our car, Daddy offered me water and an organic dog treat. I slowly chewed the small morsel, noticing its variety of flavors. Then I spit it out.

Pffft! Microplastics!

Learning Dog Tricks

Keke attends her first meeting of the Dynamic Dog Club

Daddy belongs to a "Dynamic Dog Club." What made a *dynamic* dog club any different from any other one? I did not know because dogs were not invited to club meetings.

What's the point of a dog club without any dogs, you ask? Hmph, me too. If dogs ruled the world, things would be different. But as anyone should know, empires and rulers have come and gone over the eons, but dogs are the one constant man has always depended on. We do not rule. We *influence*.

When Daddy came home from last month's meeting, he announced that the next meeting would be different. Dogs were allowed—in fact, encouraged—to attend. The big feature of the next meeting would be "dog tricks." Humans were expected to show off their dogs' latest maneuvers.

Oh, no. Please, just no.

Trick *and* treat

I've sniffed out this trail before and know where it leads. Mommy and Daddy have tried to teach me tricks in the past, and it didn't end well.

Don't get me wrong: I'm not afraid to try new things. I'm also not a stuck-up kitty-cat who refuses to perform under any conditions. So, a long time ago, when they wanted to teach me to "sit," I thought, no big deal, I got this.

My humans have said before that I am not a food-motivated dog. The truth is, I like a rare T-bone as much as the next dog, but that's not what they were offering. Half the time, they forgot to bring the treats, so they asked me to do tricks with the promise that they would later produce the treats. And then they forgot the promise.

The other half of the time, they brought a pathetic, crunchy store-bought treat with all the pleasant aroma of wet socks after a rainy walk. Ultimately, I agreed to pee outside, and they stopped trying to teach me tricks. Beyond that, we agreed to disagree.

Roll over, Beethoven

So this month, when Daddy announced he would teach me to roll over, a trick we hadn't attempted before, I was skeptical but thought, okay, we'll give it a try. After all, what did we have to lose besides wet-sock-infused pupperonis, our already-frazzled nerves, and all sense of dignity and decorum?

I won't bore you with details, but let's just say it was less than stellar. And I don't want to point fingers, but somebody couldn't decide the starting position, which way to roll, or when to stop.

The dog club meeting

Finally, the day of the dog club meeting arrived. I'd forgotten all about it, assuming I wouldn't be going since our "trick training" had been such a flop. Apparently, Daddy had other ideas, and Mommy was in on it. She bathed and brushed me, and then they took me on "a fun car ride to meet the other puppies." Hmmm. I'd heard that phrase before we headed out to the dog park once last year. (See the lesson of that name from my previous book, *The Dog Park Massacre*—the name says it all.) Needless to say, I was cautious.

The ride was short, and they led me to a building I'd never been to. I could hear dogs yapping and woofing before the door opened. We entered a large room with seats around the perimeter, and the interior a veritable smorgasbord of dogs of every size, scent, and breed. There were so many to meet, all on leashes, and the majority were surprisingly friendly.

After introductions, the meeting was called to order, and we settled down. Daddy picked me up, to my chagrin. I wanted to say a few more words to that cute Pomeranian.

One by one, dogs were brought to the center of the room to perform their tricks. We watched as a Golden Retriever played "Nose Touch." A Poodle "crawled" and then took a bow. But my favorite was a Yorkie that flipped in mid-air to a round of thunderous applause.

All this left me wondering, why was I here? Had Mommy and Daddy brought me to show me what other dogs could do? To shame me for not learning a trick?

My anxieties peaked when Daddy carried me to the center of the room and announced that Keke would perform a new trick, something no one had seen today.

What are you talking about, Daddy? We never discussed this!

I gave him a low growl and my best stink-eye look as he introduced me as the author of my blog, *Keke's Guide to Training Your Human.* He then explained to all that I was not a food-motivated dog. No, he said, I only responded to love. True enough, but where was this leading? I tried to warn him he was barking up the wrong tree if he thought I might spontaneously transform into a professional gymnast.

Yet he proceeded, even asking the audience to practice showing me love by saying, in unison, "Good girl, Keke!" He told everyone they needn't worry about visibility because I would do the trick from his hands.

Really, Daddy? Are you barking mad?

And that's when it occurred to me: perhaps he planned to throw me in the air and flip me like a Yorkshire pancake!

I half expected a drum roll as the room fell silent and all eyes focused on me. Then he lifted me above his head the way Rafiki displayed the newborn Lion King and proudly commanded, "Keke, look cute!"

There was much laughter before everyone said in unison, "Good girl, Keke!"

Very funny, Daddy. I'd be LOL if I weren't TOF (Teeth On Finger).

The Headbangers Ball

Sneaky-Keke vs. Squirmy-Wormy

Ah, the sweet smells of spring after an overnight rain: fresh earth, crocuses poking their heads up, and worms strewn across the sidewalk like leftover spaghetti at a toddler's birthday party.

Daddy and I were on our morning walk, and the ground was alive with *squirmy-wormies*. Not the sluggish, boring worms from up north—no, sir. Down here, we've got jumping worms, the Cirque du Soleil of the worm world. All it takes is one little nudge from me, and *BOING*! They flip and flop like fish on a trampoline.

After ten feet, I had five worms wriggling in my wake. I felt like a parade leader—except instead of a marching band, I had a silent, squishy percussion section.

Daddy, of course, didn't appreciate my artistry.

"Leave those disgusting worms alone!" he barked.

Disgusting? Really, Daddy? They smell like fresh potato peels! And you eat things from the ground all the time—onions, turnips, five-second-rule chocolates. At least I have standards.

Just as I was about to launch into a speech on worm appreciation, I heard a *rat-a-tat-tat* from overhead. I looked up, and there it was: a woodpecker going full maniac on a tree.

Why would anyone choose to smash their face into a tree? Repeatedly?

Daddy followed my gaze. "Ah, a woodpecker!" he said. "Another creature who likes worms. Though he prefers the non-squirmy, tree-stuffed kind—grubs."

He paused thoughtfully.

"Reminds me of the pelicans at the beach."

Interesting analogy. Both bash their heads looking for snacks. Maybe they have a support group.

Then Daddy launched into one of his... poems.

Not again.

The Pelican Dive

The pelican soars on mighty wings,

Scanning below for fishy things.

With a tuck and a roll and a mighty splash,

The fish swim away in a high-tailing dash!

I thought such an impact might give you some traction
     time.

Instead, the head pounding dulled your reaction time.

If you want to catch fish before they've all fled, dear —

Perhaps you'll consider the wearing of headgear!

Sigh.

Not terrible. Not Ogden Nash. But not terrible.

Anyway, back to my parade.

I stalked a particularly juicy, squirmy-wormy, my tail high, my nose twitching like a bushy-tailed woodpecker ready to strike.

"Play with me!" I barked.

"Catch me if you can!" the worm taunted, flipping end over end.

Just as I made my move—yank! My leash jerked me back like a fishing line.

Foiled again!

Geez, Daddy, I'm banging my head against the wall! At this rate, I'll have a tunnel to the neighbor's yard by Tuesday!

Happy Birthday, Keke!

The ultimate guide to celebrating ME

Can you believe it? April 20th will be my birthday!

I know what you're thinking: "OF COURSE I know Keke's birthday is coming up! I've had it marked with golden milk bones on my calendar because I'd never want to miss the biggest celebration day EV-ER! Because what could be more important than the day when the cutest, funniest, and funnest puppy in the world turns a year older?"

I'm sure you have all kinds of plans, gifts, and party schemes in mind. Still, just in case you're a few ideas short, I've compiled this handy guide to ensure you make my special day the most spectacular possible.

1. Pamper me like royalty

Let's start with the basics. I expect the royal treatment from sunrise to sunset and beyond. You can begin my day with a luxurious bath featuring organic, lavender-infused Paw de Luxe shampoo (none of that generic stuff, please), followed by a fluffy towel wrap and gentle blow-dry. And don't forget the post-bath massage, complete with Black Cherry Merlot paw balm.

2. Fashion-forward

No birthday would be complete without the perfect outfit. I envision a bespoke ensemble tailored to showcase my impeccable sense of style. Think designer doggy couture, complete with sparkling accessories like a bejeweled collar and a silver tiara. Something befitting my status as the reigning darling diva.

3. Culinary delights fit for a queen

A true celebration requires gourmet cuisine, and I have discerning tastes. Whip up a feast for royalty, featuring my favorite dishes—perhaps some succulent, grass-fed steak with Béarnaise sauce accompanied by Potatoes Lyonnaise. And let's not forget the pièce de résistance: a delectable bacon-flavored birthday cake adorned with edible flowers and personalized with my name in pink frosting.

4. Walks in the most spectacular places

For my birthday walks, I expect only the most bougie places, accompanied by fashionable celebrities like Gonker from *Dog Gone*, Mickey's friend Pluto, and, of course, Taylor Swift. I'm thinking maybe a special parade down Main Street, U.S.A., in the Magic Kingdom, with yours truly flanked on both sides by Disney stars of all eras.

Speaking of Eras, I can jet-set to Paris in the evening for a walk down the Champs-Élysées with Taylor. She'll want to give me a personal tour of her favorite shops, such as Louis Vuitton, Hermès, and Dior. I'm flexible; whatever Tay wants. It doesn't all have to be about me.

JUST KIDDING—of course it does!

5. Paw-some entertainment

After we explore the glittery shops of Paris, I expect Tay will want to give a personal performance just for me and a few hundred of my closest friends, ending with her and her surprise guests singing "Happy Birthday Dear Keke" in four-part harmony. Since I have diverse tastes, consider adding Ed Sheeran, Morgan Wallen, and Nicki Minaj. It should be no big deal for my besties to arrange, right?

6. Gifts galore

Last but certainly not least, let's talk presents. Now, this is where you, dear readers, can shine. I have compiled a meticulously curated wishlist on Pinterest that is guaranteed to make my tail wag. The options are endless, from plush toys and gourmet treats to stylish accessories and cozy beds. Just remember, it's the thought that counts—as long as you wrap each gift with love (and adoration). And make it the crunchy kind of wrapping paper so it's more fun to shred!

So there you have it, devoted followers—the ultimate guide to celebrating Keke in all her glory. As my birthday approaches, I trust you will spare no expense in ensuring every moment is tailored to my liking. After all, a puppy of my caliber deserves nothing but the best. Now, let the countdown to the most memorable birthday bash of the year be unleashed!

I'm Not So Hot About Growing Up

You still call the shots

There are many dull hours at our house. After the perimeter has been patrolled for signs of intruders and the house inspected for overlooked crumbs, I spend much tedious time doing nothing.

Sometimes, however, a down day with little to do can be precisely what's needed. Today, I am not feeling so well. I am tired, my belly hurts, and I only want to curl up in a corner of the couch. Mommy and Daddy keep my favorite comfy blanket there—the soft white one with the little dog prints—and I retire to my spot.

Still, I'm not feeling so badly that it stops me from jumping up and barking the moment the doorbell rings. Or running to get my soccer ball as soon as Liam enters the door. Liam is the oldest of three boys who invaded my house last Thanksgiving, and Mommy is still recovering. This time, fortunately, it's just him and his mother.

Hearing my barks and seeing my soccer ball, Liam engages and kicks the ball into the family room. I run after it and hit the ball with my head, then realize I'm feeling woozy and return to my spot on the couch.

Liam follows, ready for soccer, but turns when he sees me on the couch.

"Hey, Keke," he says, sitting next to me and gently patting my head. "You okay?"

I appreciate his concern, and I rise to let him pet me.

Liam sucks in a breath and calls out. "Hey, Mom, I think something's wrong with Keke."

As Liam's mother and my Mommy come to the couch, Liam adds, "She's bleeding."

Shocked, I look behind me where I had lain, and sure enough, there is a dark spot on the white blanket.

It is Mommy's turn for concern. She rolls me over, inspects my belly, and then says, "Keke's okay, Liam. She's just going through something called 'heat,' which is a normal part of being a girl dog."

Liam still looks worried, so Mommy continues. She tells him female dogs go through heat cycles, during which they may feel tired and uncomfortable and have symptoms like bleeding.

Turning to me, she says, "You'll be okay, Keke. It's nothing to worry about. You'll be back up and playing soccer in no time. Right now, if you don't feel well, rest."

Whew! I appreciate Mommy's assurances. I let Liam pet me some more, and he spends most of the afternoon with me. We even take a nap together on the couch.

After Liam leaves, I lie on the couch, my mind racing. Is this what it's like to grow up? If "heat cycles" are part of being a big dog, what choice do I have? And what other mysteries await me on the road to becoming a dog?

I look down and spy a tissue on the floor. I remember last year when I couldn't get down from the couch without my humans helping me because the couch was guarded by the "scary stairs." Now, however, I am a big puppy who can climb the stairs to the couch without a second thought.

I look at the floor again and marvel at how close the ground is and how far away it seemed when I first viewed it from this perch. I have grown larger since then, but not much. I mostly overcame my fears.

I descend to the floor, grab the tissue with my teeth, and start to chew it. Piece by tiny piece, I shred the tissue until it is a pile of pulp.

Satisfied, I climb the steps and return to my favorite spot on the couch.

That will show them. Keke, the puppy, is still calling the shots!

At the Lake
(Part 1 of Vacation Getaways)

Bullfrogs, leeches, and bass teeth

They promised this was going to be an epic vacation. Lounging by the lake, meeting puppies and distant friends and relatives, visiting exotic new places to sniff and poop.

They believe all I think about is sniffing and pooping, but humans have no idea the depth of canine thoughts. And it's not surprising. After all, what kind of original ideas would you expect from the breed that concocted over a hundred varieties of Oreo cookies?

* * *

153 hours and 1,436 "Are we there yet?" whines later, we arrived at the lake house.

The sun was nearing the horizon. The air was heavy with the smell of aquatic life: ducks, fish, bullfrogs, and something familiar that took a moment to put my nose on.

Of course—bullfrog poop.

The lake was calm, disturbed only by the odd dragonfly flitting over the water and the occasional fish tail breaking the surface. From the look of those tails, some of them would be right at home in Loch Ness.

There were also cattails by the waterside. But where were the cats?

The highlight of the lake house was a screened deck as large as the rest of the house. It had furniture for humans and a large pillow on the floor for me. And the view! The deck stood over the water like a Great Dane, and the screened walls were floor-to-ceiling, allowing me to look over the lake and watch for ships and sea monsters.

The owners of this cabin thought of everything!

That evening, a storm erupted. The wind came first, then large raindrops pelted the house in slow, indifferent patterns. Each drop of rain sounded like a frog jumping on the metal roof of the deck. After a few minutes, their hops quickened, and before long, a truckload of croaking amphibians bounced and blended.

In the distance, lightning crackled and lit up the sky. It was followed by a slow-rolling grumble, like my stomach waiting for Mommy and Daddy to finish dinner.

That night, I dreamed of an army of bullfrogs guarding our cabin, their croaks echoing in perfect harmony. "Hup, two, three, four," they chanted as they marched in unison, their eyes gleaming with a mysterious determination.

* * *

The following morning, the sun brightened the sky like the storm had never happened. Daddy pulled an old canoe from the side of the house. Mommy and I donned life jackets, and we took to sea.

The sun, initially warm and inviting, turned hot as the afternoon progressed. Seeing me panting, Daddy picked me up and dangled me overboard with promises to cool me down.

Did I want to walk the plank? A walk would be lovely, but I don't think that's what you have in mind. I saw the giant monsters swimming in this water!

In typical fashion, Daddy mistook my protests for enthusiasm and hoisted me over the water as a ten-foot-long bass circled below. There's a reason they call them "largemouth."

Hey, fishie! I wanted you to know I'm a fishing lure, and I have a giant hook ready to spear you if you bite me!

Daddy lowered me into the cool water, and I immediately turned and swam back to the boat, bumping noses with the canoe. Eventually, Daddy decided my tortures were over. I felt better once I was in the canoe and had shaken loose all the leeches and bass teeth from my body. Humans wonder why dogs always shake after they get wet—now you know. Leeches and bass teeth.

Returning to shore, I had dinner, played soccer on the porch, took a late-night walk, and then collapsed into bed and slept like a log. Or a dog. Whatever.

* * *

The next morning, we rose early and packed the car with all our belongings. It was time to continue our trek north to our next exciting adventure, and there was no time to lose.

I waved goodbye as a chorus of bullfrogs croaked, "So long, farewell."

Their performance was *ribbeting*.

To be continued...

The Next Stop
(Part 2 of Vacation Getaways)

Don't forget to take your vacation hall pass

I love vacations. The thrill of discovering new places, meeting fascinating new people, dogs, and even unsuspecting wildlife. The sheer delight of sniffing scents my nose has never known. The joy of pushing the boundaries of human patience.

And pups, let's be real—there's a reason they call it a getaway. It's your golden opportunity to expand your horizons and *get away* with things that would usually land you in a poopload of trouble.

Besides, humans *want* their vacations to be relaxing and stress-free. That means they're far more likely to excuse transgressions, explain away undesirable conduct, and dream up new ways to anthropomorphize their pets. It's like they pack extra patience along with the sunscreen.

Stretching the limits

Getting away with mischief on vacation is like having a hall pass—it grants you extra freedom, but there are limits. Push too far, and you'll find yourself in the principal's office. Or worse—solitary confinement.

Let me share my travel tale—the one where I boldly test the outermost edges of vacation leniency. As always, I take the risks and learn the lessons so my loyal followers don't have to.

You lucky dogs!

The hall pass

I usually let Mommy and Daddy sleep in my bed at night (although my claims of dominion have been disputed).

In our regular home, stairs allow me to get on and off the bed whenever needed. I have a pee pad in the bedroom, so I don't have to wake anybody in the middle of the night. I climb down, take care of business, and climb back up. No muss, no fuss. Everyone is happy.

Trouble arose on this stop of our vacation because somebody forgot to pack my stairs. I don't want to be a snitch, but the guilty party's name starts with a 'D' and ends with a 'Y'.

Consequently, when the urge struck in the middle of the night, the party of the first part had only two options: she could bark and wake the party of the second part, or take care of things independently.

The other problem with our vacation home was that the sleepable real estate was smaller than usual. Decreased lot size means increased property disputes, and the biggest foot usually wins. So I was already feeling peevish about my loss of autonomy and freehold when the 4 AM bladder call woke me.

I saw this night's stopover location as a logical place to stake my ownership claim. I wasn't greedy. I didn't want much territory—I'm a compact dog with small needs. So I limited my territorial declaration to a small corner on Mommy's side of the bed, which at the time was foot-free. And I asserted my claim atop a fluffy and apparently absorbent bedspread.

Either I overestimated bedcover absorbency or underestimated bladder capacity. All I know is that Mommy discovered my claim in short order.

Here, I must pause my story and warn you: there are better times than 4 AM for a calm evaluation of competing claims. The aftereffects of adult beverages have worn off, the coffee is still at least three hours away from brewing, and the judge is not feeling particularly lenient.

So, I played my hall pass card, adding some affectionate pleas of sorrow.

Friends, let me tell you, the gambit was a success! Mommy covered the sheets with absorbent towels, we all went back to sleep, and level heads prevailed over the extra laundry in the morning. All parties agreed that the arrangements were strange, new, and deserving of special status.

The following night, primal urges once again led to squirting splurges, but unfortunately, with a different outcome. This time, pleas for parley and leniency were dismissed with prejudice. I was served an eviction notice without due process, followed by the unthinkable: I was incarcerated in the dreaded "crate" for the remainder of the night without food, water, or a single phone call. No Miranda rights were read, and requests for legal representation were ignored. I do not hold out high hopes of appeal since this was obviously the work of a sham court with judicial bias.

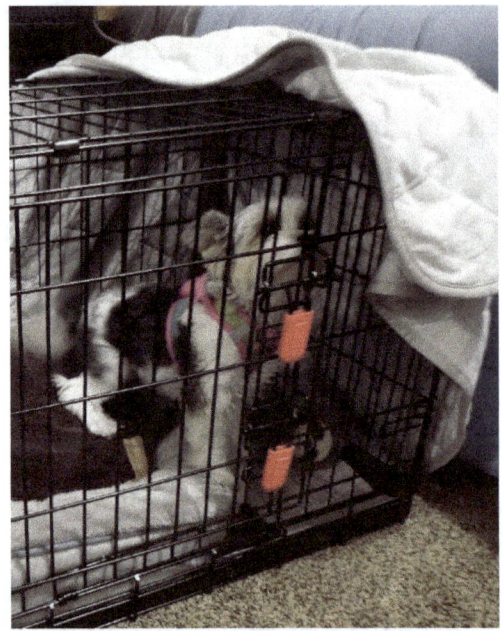

In retrospect, I should have checked my hall pass reusability and exclusion terms.

My advice: Wait two days minimum before trying to reinvoke your hall pass.

To be continued...

Dog On It
(Part 3 of Vacation Getaways)

Vacationing can be dangerous…
unless you have a dog

After a prolonged drive, we arrived at our next vacation stop. Traveling to new places can be exciting but also dangerous, like my trip to the beach last year when I nearly drowned but was rescued by an alert dolphin.

This destination was very different from our first one. Instead of a peaceful cottage by a lake, we stayed in a small city in a multi-floor apartment building. The exterior was modern brick, yet an old church steeple topped the structure, peering down like an evil eye. Across the road was an ancient cemetery with overgrown weeds and toppled headstones. What happens to a grave's inhabitants when their monument is displaced? There may be unseen forces and dark magic that require a dog's advanced senses. More on that later.

The building was heavily fortified, leaving me to wonder what secrets it guarded.

First, Mommy entered a keypad code to gain access. Then, we transited a narrow hall and a heavy steel door to another passageway. I went first, boldly leading my family into the dark abyss, only to be blinded by bright lights a moment later as my humans followed.

Double doors on the left slid silently open, and Daddy entered a tiny room, beckoning me to follow. The floor smelled like a crime scene of past occupants—some human, some canine, and at least one who might have been a rogue skunk in disguise. I tried to make a run for it, but the doors shut faster than a toddler chasing an ice cream truck, narrowly missing my delicate snout.

I inspected the tiny room, my heart drumming like a caffeinated Chihuahua. It was a shiny steel prison with suspiciously smooth walls that offered no escape routes, only a railing at human height—clearly useless for someone of my stature. The only thing breaking the monotony was a panel of mysterious buttons next to the doors. Daddy pressed one, and suddenly the floor shuddered like it had a personal vendetta.

I suddenly felt very heavy, and it seemed like a giant tornado had snatched the whole room and lifted it off the ground. I was Toto, and Daddy was Dorothy, except there was no Kansas at the end of this nightmare, and Daddy wasn't wearing a cute blue bonnet. We were trapped in a metal box of doom.

As the room creaked and groaned, I crouched low to the floor to keep my balance. Pity the poor humans who had only two legs.

A minute later, the doors reopened, and I stared into a hallway identical to the one we had just left. My humans may have been tricked into thinking we were in the same place, but I could smell the deception. We were in a different place—or was it a different time? Would we find evil witches and flying monkeys in an alternate universe, or an unholy scientist with a time machine?

Mommy led us into the passageway, oblivious to the perils surrounding her.

In my limited time on Earth, I've realized that humans' deficient faculties make them blind to many threats. The astute ones acknowledge their limitations and seek the assistance of vigilant canines like me. The truly wise ones heed our warnings.

Mine, unfortunately, did not fall into either category that day. Something sinister had happened inside that little steel room—something only I recognized.

I needed to warn my humans of the trap. I strained at my leash and barked. But Daddy's only response was a perky, "C'mon Keke!"

Did I mention they were oblivious? They hired me for a purpose, yet ignored my superior senses. I would have to be doubly alert. I could not depend on scarecrows, lions, or tin men to rescue us.

Across the narrow hall, another passcode gave entry to what would be our temporary home. It was a discomforting place, eerie like the cemetery and the tornado room. Creatures danced on our ceiling. Late-night visitors spoke in hushed tones outside our door but never knocked. My barks of warning were met only with, "Keke, hush!"

The next two weeks were a whirlwind as I was shuttled from dog crate to car to strange houses. I felt like Toto spinning down the Yellow Brick Road, always watching for flying monkeys.

The trip had its moments—some exciting, some tolerable, and some that smelled suspiciously like betrayal. But nothing compared to the sweet relief of repacking the car and heading to our next destination, where I could finally stop sniffing for hidden perils at every turn.

I've heard that some humans leave their patrol dogs behind when they go on vacation. It's a miracle any of these humans make it home without being kidnapped by barn owls or ambushed by rogue mail carriers.

To be continued...

Building Character
(Conclusion of Vacation Getaways)

A well-timed messin' will teach them a lesson

After bidding a not-so-fond farewell to the noisy apartment with alternate universes, we headed for the next stopover, the mid-point on our journey home. It was another all-day drive, which I endured with my usual calm demeanor and alacrity.

Hey, I heard that. Keep your comments to yourself, please. This is my story, and I'll tell it how I want.

After hundreds of hours of driving, we arrived at our next destination: a lakeside house where we would be the guests of honor. This time, a proper welcoming committee greeted us, including a friendly Beagle-mix named Chester, two wide-eyed cats who kept a respectful distance, and a couple of high-ranking nobles sent to greet her ladyship. Unlike our prior stops, the humans understood the nuances of welcoming visiting dignitaries and influential canines. The nobles genuflected and recognized my royal cuteness.

The back porch was like a private theater, complete with two bubbling ponds and waterfalls that gurgled a soothing soundtrack. The star performers? Goldfish so enormous their heads could moonlight as bowling balls. They were friendly and inquisitive, and I was certain they'd make fantastic playmates, darting about in their glittery costumes. Their lips moved, apparently saying "wa-wa," but even with my extended range of hearing, I couldn't fathom their words. What could they want? A drink of water?

But when I asked Daddy to fetch one for me, he just rolled his eyes and muttered something about "boundaries." Humans, honestly—they can be such wet blankets.

The following day, it was dé·jà vu as Mommy dressed me in my lifejacket. Daddy pulled two kayaks to the murky water's edge. Thoughts of our prior canoe-paddling experience swam through my head like a largemouth bass.

It was shaping up into another one of Daddy's patented outdoor torture lessons—because apparently, "building character" involves testing my survival instincts. What's next, tightrope walking over a pit of alligators?

Mommy and I bobbed along in our kayak, resembling a turtle lost in a sea of turbocharged bunnies. She waved to frolicsome children who screamed and bounced on inflated rafts dragged behind zippy speedboats like an endless game of tag.

"Hey, how about one of those speedboats instead of this wobbly coffin?" I asked. But nooo, fun and character building are apparently mortal enemies.

Daddy had other plans. His idea of a "good time" involved plopping me into the water and watching as I navigated between jellyfish and great white sharks. I'm pretty sure he was hoping I'd end up on some kind of Guinness World Records page as the first tiny dog to paddle the English Channel. He wanted to know if I was having "fun" yet.

You keep using that word. I do not think it means what you think it means.

After hundreds of harrowing hours lost at sea, we finally staggered back to solid ground, parched, emaciated, and with ribs so extended I resembled a tiny dino skeleton.

That night, the indignities continued. The "runnies" kept me up, turning pee pads and blankets into an artistic Rorschach built with canine suffering. By morning, my humans were so rattled they packed the car in record time and took turns riding in the back seat with me, ready to spring into action at the first sign of gastrointestinal rebellion.

When we arrived home, they presented me with a peace offering of roast chicken and rice to soothe my delicate stomach. I felt perfectly fine by then, but why let the truth ruin a perfectly good meal? Extending the pity party is just smart strategy—how else will they learn their lesson?

That'll teach them to toss me in the lake!

Happy Father's Day From the Cat

Letters from the Litter Box: Observing Canine Chaos

Dear reader: Sunday was Father's Day in the U.S., and Daddy received a t-shirt from Zoey, the cat who lives in our spare bedroom. The shirt was accompanied by the following letter, which I found humorous and bordering on truthful. I am, therefore, publishing it below without alteration. Yours, Keke

Dear Daddy,

Today, I present a t-shirt that captures the pleasures of your relationship with the playful family pup, Keke. Life wouldn't be the same without her slobbery kisses and purposeful ignorance of your commands. And how could I possibly contain my excitement over another day of her endless barking and tireless enthusiasm?

I so admire her aptitude for greeting you with total devotion and suicidal fervor. There is nothing more exciting than watching a game of puppy roulette as she jumps about the top of the couch with wild abandon, challenging the ability of gravity to send her toppling to the floor while expressing her undying faithfulness.

Your attempts to stifle her excitement—as well as her barking—are equally entertaining, as she hangs upon your every command. (The scene could only be improved by attaching her leash to the ceiling fan so we might see her hanging elsewhere, too.)

Then there is the obligatory walk, which you and Keke must immediately embark upon after your return. The scene at the front door, in which you attempt to attach the leash while she alternates between licking your hands and jumping in excitement, makes for great fun. The canine saliva on your fingers makes it impossible for you to grip the metal mechanism to clip the leash, and the result is that you both spend more time by the door than her bladder can withstand. Oops!

I am only a humble entertained visitor in this comic adventure, but I appreciate the opportunity to witness the farce.

From my foremost window observation perch, I have front-row seats at the start of the walk. Keke's ability to turn every stroll into a grand adventure is nothing short of impressive. I mean, who wouldn't want to sniff every blade of grass and mark every tree in the yard?

I have seen it take twenty minutes for you to drag our little darling the fifteen feet it takes to reach the curb, prodding her with ambiguous commands like, "Keke, come!"

Such thrilling escapades, really. Riveting entertainment.

Once you return from your fruitful hike, there is nothing I love better than watching the two of you play games. Fetch is one of my favorites.

A ball, a stuffy, my favorite toy mouse—nothing is safe from her relentless pursuit. It's almost as if she believes she's doing me a favor by returning my carefully hidden treasures. Spoiler alert: she's not.

Her loyalty and energy are something to behold. I mean, who else could be so thrilled by the same monotonous routine day in and day out? It's a talent, really. Personally, I enjoy my independence and selective affection, but hey, to each their own.

Despite our differences, I relish the peculiar détente between Keke and me. She tolerates my well-deserved superior attitude, and I tolerate her less-refined nature. It's almost charming, in a way. (Just don't get me started on her palate.)

So Happy Father's Day, Daddy. I hope you continue to enjoy your faithful companion, the persistent, tail-wagging, overly exuberant hairball that she is. Life would be dreadfully dull without her comic antics, her ceaseless need for attention, and your persistent belief that she will someday "calm down."

Meanwhile, I'm still here, maintaining my dignity, and enjoying my nap.

Sincerely (or as sincerely as a cat can muster), Zoey

Shear Madness

Grooming matters: A hair above the rest

News flash: We are immersed in a battle called the great hypoallergenic debate. The lines are drawn, with fur on one side and hair on the other.

Welcome to the battlefield of a clash as heated as a back-alley catfight. On one side, we have the fur-flying faction, and on the other, the hair-growing heroes. Some humans insist that the ideal dog doesn't shed, while others balk at the idea of shelling out a hundred dollars a month for grooming (as if their own trips to the salon are a bargain). Then there's the wildcard camp: those who prefer hairless dogs that look like rats straight from the sewers of the Bronx.

Furball or hairball?

Despite what some humans believe, dog "hair" and "fur" are made of the same thing: keratin. Shocking, I know. But hair—like mine—has a luxurious, silky feel that fur simply can't match. Admit it, you love petting hair dogs like me. We're irresistibly soft, like living plush toys.

However, many of the so-called "furballs" sport a double coat of fur. Think Golden Retrievers, Siberian Huskies, or Double-Stuff Oreos that have rolled through the cat's bed.

The undercoat is soft and delicate—almost as soft as me—while the outer coat is coarse and rough, like an old doormat. Let's be honest, would you rather pet a doormat or a nice, soft hairball?

Uh, I mean, a long-haired dog. Definitely not a hairball.

Dander

Allergies aren't caused by what your dog's fur is made of—they're triggered by how often that fur sheds. And here's the kicker: "fur" tends to fall out far more often than "hair."

It's not the keratin you're sneezing over—it's the dead skin cells, or dander, hitching a ride on the fur.

Dead skin! There's nothing dandy about that.

So, if you're a human battling allergies, how do you choose your canine companion?

Here's my advice: The ideal dog is the one staring up at you with those soulful eyes, tail wagging furiously.

Bring home the cutest, most lovable puppy you can find, and let the allergy pills do their thing. A nice glass of Chardonnay will help, too—it pairs wonderfully with unconditional love.

A note about grooming

Because we long-haired dogs shed so infrequently, our hair needs to be cut regularly. I'm talking every six weeks, minimum. Otherwise, I get hot, itchy, and—let's be honest—cranky.

So, what happens when my humans decide to save a few bucks and give me a hatchet-job home grooming instead of springing for a professional?

Let's just say the dark spot on the carpet speaks volumes.

Being Ghosted

You don't have to be a hot dog to howl

Please, never say those four words. She said them with innocence, in a bright and cheery voice. But I knew their deeper, darker meaning. Words I never want to hear:

"Be a good girl."

Mommy only says them when she's leaving me. And as she approached the door, I cried. I barked. I howled.

Oh, why oh why did I howl? I didn't mean to. *My faux paw.*

Some dogs tell me we're all good howlers—that it's in our genes—but I don't believe them. (Humans, on the other paw, are good liars. It's definitely in *their* genes.)

I wish I could howl like Liesel, the Dachshund from down the street, who sounds like an opera singer auditioning for the part of "Heartbroken Pup No. 1." My howl comes out as a string of staccato barks—more like a malfunctioning squeaky toy. Nobody feels sorry for me. Liesel gets sympathetic ear scratches, but I get imitations. *Hysterical—not.*

Maybe if I were a better howler, she wouldn't leave.

But Mommy just turned to me and said, "You'll be okay. I won't be long."

As I heard the car backing out of the garage, my despair grew. It was like the trip to the dog park when all the puppies piled on "the new kid," and I was stuck on the bottom of the heap, helpless. Only this time, I was *alone* and helpless.

I ran to the living room and climbed to my overlook at the back of the couch. From there, I could survey the lonely desolation that surrounded me. Nothing moved. I looked out the window at the trees, hoping for some sign of life to distract me, but the whole world seemed to be taking a nap. No squirrels playing their acrobatic version of tag, no birds fussing over nest renovations, and no breeze to ruffle the leaves. It was so still that I half-expected a tumbleweed to roll by and a cowboy to whistle in the distance.

I looked around for my friend, Mousey. He was usually near my toy basket on the floor by the couch, but today, he wasn't there. Nobody was.

Why did Mommy leave me alone like this? Had I been bad? Was I being punished?

I groaned. This wasn't normal. She usually put me in the crate when she left me alone—a cozy little box of safety and zero temptation. At least there, I couldn't get into trouble. Everything inside was mine, and believe me, I've already destroyed most of it.

I looked at the floor and saw her white sock, the one with the pink stripe. Why did I chew her sock this morning? Had I made her so mad that she left for good, never to return? How could I be so thoughtless? So stupid?

And now I was all alone. No Mommy, no Daddy, no Mousey. Just me and my growing need to chew on something—anything.

Oh! I remembered the chew stick. It was on the bed, my salvation in these dark times. I leapt down from the couch and trotted to the bedroom with purpose. But when I got there... the door was closed. Why was the bedroom door closed? What kind of monster would do this to me?

Panic set in. I sprinted to the living room, picked up Mommy's sock, and bounded to the top of the couch in three steps. The only sound in the room was my heavy breathing. Even the refrigerator had stopped humming.

Was this some kind of test? Did she want to see just how much chaos I could unleash in her absence? Or maybe it was a chance to prove I could be responsible. But then again, what if she never came back? What if she'd left me with just food, water, and a couple of pee-pee pads, planning for the neighbors to find my decaying body days from now, like some tragic hero of a canine survival story?

I lay down and closed my eyes to squeeze back the tears.

I had the sock in my mouth, so I chewed it, focusing on the pink stripe. I held down one end with my paw and pulled the other with my teeth. The more I bit into the soft cloth, the better I felt. It made me forget my loneliness. My eyes drooped, and I let myself imagine I was chewing a juicy steak.

* * *

I awoke with a start. There were noises outside the house. I opened my mouth to bark but was startled by something wet hitting my paw. I looked down in confusion. It was Mommy's sock— or at least, what was left of it. There was a large hole in the frayed fabric, a two-inch gash in the pink stripe. If Mommy had a dewclaw—that fifth claw that dogs have above the paw—this hole would've been a perfect fit for it to stick out.

But Mommy didn't have a dewclaw. She would not appreciate my "helpful redesign." But what did it matter? She was never coming back anyway.

I was surprised to hear the garage door open. I growled and stood, barking repeatedly, projecting my voice. Within a minute, the door would doubtless close as the trespassers realized their error: this was not a house to burgle.

The noise was quickly replaced by the sound of a car pulling into the garage. I knew that car.

"Mommy!" I shouted, bounding from the couch and barking all the way to the garage door. A minute later, Mommy entered the house, and I ran to her, howling with glee and excitement. She'd come back!

"Whoa, whoa, okay Keke, calm down."

She picked me up, and I covered her with kisses.

I'm sorry. I'm so, so sorry about your sock! And my howling! I wish I weren't so lousy at it.

She laughed. "You sounded so pitiful when you howled like that. I hurried back as quick as I could."

At that moment, the bedroom door opened, and Daddy emerged. What was he doing here? How had he gotten into the bedroom?

Mommy was trying to hold me out of range of her love shower as she turned to Daddy. "You'd think I was gone for twenty hours instead of twenty minutes! Did you have a good nap?"

He blinked and yawned, looking at his watch. "Yeah, I guess I fell asleep. Keke, why were you making all that racket?"

Racket? Didn't you hear what she said? It's only my howling that brought her back!

Ugly Dog Sweaters and Other Indignities

At least the sweater dries

I knew the day was off to a bad start when Daddy approached me with that pink sweater—two sizes too small and adorned with ropey twists that screamed "granny chic." Despite my best evasive maneuvers, he managed to wrestle it over my head, oblivious to the fashion crime he was committing. As I stepped outside, I could almost hear the squirrels laughing from the trees, their tiny paws pointing in mockery.

But my worst nightmares were realized when I saw Boo emerge from his house across the street. Boo is equal parts Chihuahua, Bulldog, and "You wanna sniff this?"

Great. Just what I needed—a front-row audience for my fashion faux paw.

I went into full tail-tuck mode as Boo paused at the end of his driveway, eyeing me like a chew toy that squeaked "mock me." Then, with the precision of a seasoned artist, he lifted his leg and commenced his masterpiece on a garbage bag left for pickup.

Fortunately, Boo's human drew his attention away from me.

"No, Boo!" she yelled. "No peeing on the trash!"

She continued yelling, "No, no, NO!" as they crossed the street, even though Boo was no longer marking any territory. She increased the volume of her beratement as they neared the bag at the end of our driveway.

Unfortunately, as Daddy and I approached the road, the two humans started talking, dragging Boo and me closer.

Boo isn't unfriendly, but he doesn't exactly roll out the welcome mat, either. He's the canine equivalent of a closed-door policy. Back in the day, I'd greet him with a wagging tail and enough leash-straining enthusiasm to turn heads, but his indifference eventually wore me down. I keep it casual now—a polite sniff and nothing more.

Today, though, Boo surprised me with a return sniff. It was brief, perfunctory, and devoid of enthusiasm, but hey, I thought, progress. Meanwhile, our humans exchanged the usual riveting updates on the dubious accuracy of weather forecasts, Mrs. Hopkins' jungle of a garden, and other chit-chat as dry as a stale cracker left out in the sun.

And that's when disaster struck. As the humans droned on, Boo seized the opportunity to empty his internal paint can. Unfortunately, his target wasn't a lamppost, a bush, or Mrs. Hopkins' garden. No, the chosen canvas for his artistic expression was—me.

I let out a pitiful whimper, which finally got Daddy's attention. He sucked in a sharp breath and barked, "Boo!" Boo looked up innocently, his stream unwavering, as if to say, "Yes? Can I help you?"

Boo's human froze mid-sentence, then yanked his leash so hard I thought she might lift him off the ground. "I'm so sorry!" she said—directed at Daddy, of course—assuring him that Boo had never done anything like this before.

Why Daddy got the apologies instead of me, I cannot say. But if I spoke English, I might have suggested to Boo's human that this might be an excellent time to try saying, "No, Boo, NO!"

The lesson here? In the world of canine couture, sometimes you're the trendsetter, and sometimes you're just... wet.

Takin' Care of Business

What good is a job
if it keeps you from your puppy?

You humans sure are a mystery. You wake up early in the morning to shower (and do who-knows-what in that bathroom for an hour while I'm left holding my bladder). Then, after a rushed walk, you abandon me—your best friend and loyal pup—to head off to some mysterious "job." Based on the nightly complaints over dinner, I gather "employment" is just a formal excuse to moan while you chew.

And for what? You sit in a chair, staring at a glowing rectangle. You call it *work*. I call it "couch potato-ing without the crunch".

You claim you're earning money for important things, but let's talk about priorities. I sniff you when you get home, and I know exactly what's missing: snacks. If you're out there providing, where's the evidence? No kibble, no treats, not even a single stray crumb from a sandwich. *Highly* suspicious.

You say you're *bringing home the bacon*, but I'm starting to wonder if you just bring home the bacon's scent. Hey, I'm a sucker for a crispy piece of Jimmy Dean Applewood Smoked Premium, but after you spend all day trying to find it, where does it go? Not in *my* bowl.

And don't get me started on your so-called "schedule." You grumble about deadlines and meetings, but my routine is rock solid: walk at seven, breakfast at eight, snack at ten, playtime in the afternoon. Somehow, your day is so chaotic that belly rubs and ear scratches are optional? Priorities, people! Priorities!

But here's the weirdest part—some days, you actually seem to like your job. Maybe it's like when I finally catch that elusive tail. A small victory in an otherwise baffling endeavor. Hey, whatever gets you through the day.

Retirement

Then comes that long-awaited moment when you finally get your due. Heck, I make my *doo* every day, and nobody makes a big deal about it. Half a puppy treat, at best.

But I get it, your day is special. I'm talking about the day when you've finally filled the larder with enough smoked cured pork that you can quit your job and spend all day on the couch watching sports. Or Game of Thrones. (Same meat but two different flavors, eh?)

The important thing is that no one is there demanding you do their bidding, so you finally get to do what you want! And what do you do? Spend more time with me? *I don't think so.*

I recently met a neighbor who retired and decided to start flower gardening. Don't get me wrong, I appreciate her extra time outdoors, but why spend so much energy planting things she can't even eat? And she gets angry if I try digging up one of her buried bulbs!

My strategy is much simpler: dig up the yard, and voilà! Instant treasure hunt!

I know another retiree (ahem!) who spends most of his day in front of a computer banging out stories about his dog. No kidding. He hardly has time to play fetch with his best friend. (And I'm not naming names, but this is one *seriously fun* little puppy!)

Life should be about chasing balls, rolling in the grass, and stealing socks from the laundry basket. So, dear humans, when you retire, take a page from the puppy playbook and live in the NOW: Ditch the spreadsheets and word processors, embrace the slobbery kisses, and live life like every day is a walk in the park.

The Buddy System

A family affair

I was excited when Daddy told me we were visiting
Buddy. I met the Havanese several times on walks. He
was about my height, but with the kind of girth that
made him look like he was built for comfort, not speed.
Buddy and his human, Marilyn, were always friendly to
me, though I sometimes wondered if he thought of me as
a snack-sized version of himself.

I should have paid closer attention when Daddy held me a little longer than usual at Buddy's house when he hugged me goodbye. And I should have noticed the reassuring tone in Marilyn's voice when she told me I'd be fine. But there was no time to think about it. Buddy was holding his squeaky tennis ball and waiting for me to play.

"I like your tennis ball," I said, breathless, when we took a break a little later. "Yours smells like a blend of old socks, mystery meat from under the couch, and a hint of last week's garbage. Wonderful! And it squeaks louder than any I ever heard."

"Every tennis ball is legally required to squeak," Buddy said. "But some are defective and get recalled by the Bureau of Canine Standards."

"Oh. But what about the human game of tennis? Their balls don't squeak."

"They play with the rejects," Buddy assured me.

"Really?" I said. "Where'd you learn that?"

"The Internet. You know Al Gore's dog invented it, don't you?"

"But what about—"

"We call it the 'Interwoof,' but humans got the whole thing wrong. That's why we sniff everything; we're just downloading updates."

I briefly pondered his words, but Marilyn interrupted, calling us for a walk.

That night, Marilyn fed us dinner, took us for a brief pee break, and then corraled us for bedtime.

"But where's Mommy and Daddy?" I asked.

"You live with us now," Buddy said. "Marilyn's your new Mommy."

"You and Marilyn are nice, but I miss my Mommy and Daddy," I sniffed. "And my squeaky Lambchop."

"Oh, don't worry, your humans will write when they have time."

"Write? But when—"

"And don't get upset if your letters take a while to arrive. Cats secretly run the postal service, you know. That's why your mail sometimes smells like fish."

I was still trying to process all that had happened that day when we curled up to sleep on Marilyn's bed. I tossed and turned, trying to get comfortable.

"Pssst," Buddy whispered. "If you're having trouble sleeping, I can tell you a bedtime story."

"That sounds nice," I said.

But somehow, I still had trouble sleeping after he recounted "The Legend of the Invisible Mailman," a story about a ghostly mailman who never rang the doorbell but left mysterious smells on the porch, driving dogs mad because they could never catch him. His squeaky shoes can still be heard on foggy mornings.

* * *

The next several days flew by like a dust cloud. I was constantly busy between Marilyn's long walks, frequent visits from her neighbors, and Buddy's tireless supply of stories and new facts.

One afternoon, Buddy took me on a grand tour of his territory. "See this patch of grass?" he asked. "This is the official training grounds for Olympic-level Zoomies."

"Wait, there's an Olympics for dogs?"

"Of course! And Zoomies are the most prestigious event of all!" Buddy puffed out his chest. "The winner gets to take home the Golden Lambchop chew toy—and it squeaks in three different pitches."

Before I could press him for more details, Buddy had moved on to a muddy corner of his yard. "This is called the Fountain of Youth. It's always wet here, even on bright, sunny days."

I sniffed the air. "Gee, this smells like—"

"Buddy!" Marilyn called. "Stay away from there! The repairman's coming to fix that leak in the septic system next week."

"And this tree," Buddy said, moving to a higher ground, "is where Elvis the Raccoon performs his nightly acorn juggling act."

"Hmmpf," I said. "You're pulling my legs."

"You don't believe me?" Buddy asked. "Just come out here with me after supper and see for yourself."

After dinner, we agreed to a stakeout. There was a sliver of moon in a star-filled sky. Marilyn accompanied us to the backyard so she could do some stargazing.

We waited for nearly an hour before a rustling in the tree branches caught our attention. "Here he comes!" Buddy said. "Be quiet, or he won't sing."

I peered into the darkness. On the branch of Elvis' tree, I saw the dim outline of an animal. It had a pointed snout and a thin, rat-like tail.

"That's no raccoon," I said. "That's a 'possum. And he doesn't have any acorns at all."

"Oh, that's Elvis' stunt double. Sometimes, he takes a break."

"How do you know all this stuff?" I asked.

"I call it The Buddy System. Just keep your nose to the ground and your tail in the air, and you'll always have friends."

"What does that even—" I began, but Buddy walked away before I could finish my thought.

* * *

Early the following day, I was sleeping peacefully. In my dream, I saw Mommy's car pull up. Daddy emerged, walked up the path, and rang the doorbell.

I awoke with a start, realizing the doorbell had actually rung.

"Daddy!" I barked. I continued my excited barking until Marilyn let me down from the bed so I could run to the front door. But it was just the FedEx guy delivering a package.

Marilyn stepped outside as I loped back to the bedroom.

"What's wrong?" Buddy asked.

"I miss my Mommy and Daddy," I whined. "I like it here, but I miss kissing Mommy's face. Marilyn doesn't let me do that. And Daddy throws my tennis ball against the wall so hard I have to jump three feet to catch it." I sighed. "You know so much, Buddy. Can't you find some way for me to go home?"

I wailed and howled. Then I moaned until Buddy came alongside and nuzzled me. "It's okay, Keke. I think I know how to get you home."

I sniffed back tears as I looked at him.

"It's called hoarse code," he said.

"You mean I have to neigh like a horse?"

"No, no, different kind of hoarse. If you bark in the right pattern while you run zoomies, you can send a signal directly to your humans. It's an old trick from the early days of dog-human communication. A well-known fact."

It seemed odd, but what did I have to lose? "So what's the right pattern?" I asked.

"Just keep trying. You'll know it when you find it."

I zoomed and I barked, long wavering howls and short staccato bursts. I tried everything I could think of, barking until I was hoarse and zooming until I was dizzy. When I paused to take a breath, Buddy urged me on.

"Keep going, you're just getting tuned in."

After ten more minutes, the only response was the neighbor's dog barking back, "Careful! That's how the lizards summon their spaceship!"

* * *

The following day, I was awakened again by the doorbell. But this time, I did not bark. I didn't even get out of bed: just another delivery man, no doubt.

As Marilyn answered the door, I heard her exclaim, "Boy, is Keke going to be glad to see you!"

A moment later, Marilyn returned to the bedroom and swooped me up. "Look who's here!" she said.

As I spied Mommy and Daddy by the front door, it was all Marilyn could do to hold me long enough to put me down gently on the ground. I scampered into Mommy's arms and covered her with slobbery kisses.

"Did you enjoy your week with Marilyn and Buddy?" she asked. "Wait till you see what we brought you back from vacation!"

Behind me, I heard Buddy. "See Keke? I told you it would work. There were delays in the Interwoof last night, so your hoarse code took a little longer to propagate."

"Are you sure?" I asked, pausing in my wet welcome. "Maybe they were coming back for me today anyway."

"Ha!" Buddy scoffed. "Coincidence? Hardly. The Buddy System always works. You're welcome, by the way."

Reading Doggish

Sometimes I gotta espresso myself

People tell me dogs are hard to read. That our facial expressions don't change.

Really?

Humans are the ones who are baffling. One moment, their eyes are smiling, and they're telling me what a good dog I am. The next moment, their lips are curled back, and they're baring their teeth like they are readying for attack. What's that about?

If you want to read a dog's mood, you have to look beyond the face. You have to read the whole body. For all you inattentive humans, I've developed this guide to understanding dogs' expressions.

Tail Position and Movement

A wagging tail usually means I'm excited or happy, but the speed and position matter. A slow wag with a low tail may mean caution or insecurity.

How long before Daddy discovers that I chewed his favorite baseball cap that he left in the back room? Will the cat rat me out?

If I tuck my tail between my legs, it indicates fear or anxiety.

Is that the cat coming out of the back room, holding Daddy's hat?

A stiff, straight tail suggests alertness or potential aggression.

I'm gonna get that cat!

Ears

Ears standing up or forward usually signal alertness, curiosity, or excitement.

Maybe he'll think the cat did it!

If my ears are pinned back, it could mean fear, submission, or discomfort.

Wait—THAT CAT DOESN'T HAVE ANY TEETH!

If my ears droop, it means I'm sad or worried.

OMG, Daddy's Yankees cap was signed by Derek Jeter.

Eyes

Relaxed, slightly squinted eyes show that I'm content or calm.

Daddy's a Phillies fan. He doesn't really like the Yankees anyway.

A fixed, intense stare indicates I feel threatened or am preparing to defend myself.

That cat is shaking her head, waving the hat back and forth to get Daddy's attention!

If you can see the whites of my eyes—"whale eye"—it may be a sign of fear or anxiety.

Daddy inherited that cap when his father died. He will never forgive me...

Mouth

When I pull back my lips to show my teeth, it could mean aggression or fear.

I SO want to sink my teeth into that cat!

I may yawn when stressed, anxious, or unsure of a situation.

What am I going to do? That hat was one-of-a-kind.

Body Posture

A stiff or tense body might mean I'm stressed, anxious, or ready to defend myself.

Why is Daddy looking at the cat that way?

When I lower my body to the ground or curl up in a ball, I'm trying to appear small and non-threatening, indicating fear or submission.

Please don't kill me. I didn't mean to do it. It just tasted so good I couldn't stop.

When I lie on my back with my belly and neck exposed, I am being submissive and showing you I trust you.

How could you do anything to me? I'm so cute and vulnerable.

Vocalizations

Growling indicates I'm feeling threatened or uncomfortable and warning others to back off.

That cat will be so sorry if she doesn't get out of here NOW.

Whining suggests anxiety, fear, or a desire for attention.

Look at me, Daddy. Don't look at the cat!

Barking can mean a variety of things, from excitement to warning. The pitch and frequency of the bark provide clues.

Wait, that's not his Yankees cap! That's just an old hat he wears for painting. I knew it tasted too good to be Derek Jeter's.

Overall Behavior

A loose, wiggly body usually means I'm happy and comfortable.

Whew!

When I lower my front end with my rear in the air, I'm inviting play and expressing friendliness.

Get the cap from the cat, and let's play keep-away!

Conclusion

Dogs are an easy read. A page-turner. Like a Janet Evanovitch mystery.

We wag our tails. Humans only wag their tongues!

The Wizard Will See You Now

Pay no attention to that dog behind the curtain

"Prosthetics are so much more than just a leg. They're a second chance." -Derrick Campana

What if your four-legged friend has only three good legs? Maybe the fourth was deformed at birth, or it got hurt in an accident. Sure, your friend might hobble around, but running? Forget it. And to make matters worse, the neighborhood kids call him "Yardstick" because he only has three good feet.

Or maybe your best friend isn't a dog at all but a duck with just one leg. Born that way? Maybe. Lost a leg to a gator? Could happen. Either way, life isn't easy when the only move you've got is swimming in circles.

What do the dog and duck have in common?

Derrick Campana.

Derrick began his career by building new limbs ("prostheses") for humans, but later decided to focus on animals. Every day, he improves the lives of members of the animal kingdom: dogs, ducks, sheep, goats, llamas, turtles, cows, and elephants. He even helps cats.

I like sniffing day-old poop, and Derrick likes cats. We all have our questionable life choices, don't we?

Derrick's TV show, *The Wizard of Paws*, airs on BYUtv and Disney+, and in each episode, he creates prosthetic limbs and braces for animals of all sizes. He currently has more than five seasons recorded, but I'm still catching up. I want to savor every chapter.

BIONIC PETS

Marvelous Millie, a Golden Retriever with a tennis ball

In this episode, Derrick visits Lancaster, the heart of Pennsylvania's Amish country. The Amish are known for simple living, plain dress, traditional work ethics, and the rejection of modern technology. They're a lot like me, except I dress better.

Millie's humans, Lisa and Ken Hicks, are not Amish, but they live in a rural area surrounded by farms—the kind of yard where a big dog can enjoy running free.

Alas, there's not much running in Millie's life. She was born with a shriveled left front leg, so she hobbles about on her other three legs. Still, she's an enthusiastic tennis ball retriever—though her "fetch radius" is more like a small semicircle than a whole playing field.

I've seen older dogs wheeled around the neighborhood in strollers, either because their joints gave out or they lost a showdown with a speeding car. Millie, by comparison, is doing well, but she is only three years old. Derrick says even a determined three-legged dog faces challenges down the road. Her spine is misaligned, and her remaining front leg is working overtime. Eventually, it'll wear out, too.

For now, Millie doesn't let her limitations get her down. She's got the heart of a retriever, even if her range is more "retriever-lite."

Millie's human, Lisa, has her own story, having lost her left leg in a motorcycle accident in 2013. She has a prosthesis and had to deal with loss and depression in the early years after her accident.

Lisa considers Millie a kindred spirit. She smiles as she reflects on how the family Golden has brought purpose and fulfillment to her life. "Millie's got a big personality and she loves people, she loves running, she loves tennis balls. She loves life."

* * *

Derrick arrives at the job on a crisp wintry day and parks his trailer in the Hicks' front yard. He takes a plaster mold of Millie's deformed front left leg. Over the next few days, he builds a custom prosthesis for the dog. Lisa gets to choose the color and pattern for the new leg.

After her motorcycle accident, when Lisa was fitted for a prosthesis, she hid it by wearing only full-length pants. But she has learned from her journey and selects a bright pink design for Millie's new artificial leg. "Having a nice colorful pattern like this will make people a lot more comfortable with broaching the subject, 'Oh, she's wearing a prosthetic.'"

* * *

It's a cold, snowy day in Lancaster when Millie's new leg is finally ready. Derrick attaches it carefully, and the fit looks perfect. Millie puts weight on it without flinching—a promising start. But then... nothing. She hobbles along on three legs as if the shiny new prosthetic is just an awkward winter boot she doesn't want to break in. After a few minutes, she flops dramatically into the snow like a theater diva taking her final bow, overwhelmed by the challenge—or maybe just hoping someone will bring her hot cocoa and a blanket.

Derrick calls out to his fluffy white Cavachon sidekick, Henry, for assistance. Henry isn't just a companion; he's Derrick's secret weapon—"the dog behind the curtain."

"Growl at her, Henry! Tell her to get up!" I bark at the TV. But, alas, my brilliant advice goes unheard, as I'm merely watching a prerecorded show.

Henry has his own method, anyway. He's no drill sergeant—he's a motivational speaker in a fur coat. He circles Millie like a miniature coach, giving her the "you can do this" look. Slowly, Millie's heart begins to glow like embers in a winter fireplace.

And then, it happens. The spark catches, and Millie pushes herself up onto three legs. Her front left leg trembles, unsure of its new role. Tendons stretch and unused muscles awake, but still the challenge looms like an icy driveway.

Nobody warned the cowardly lion how hard this would be. Yet here she is, tapping into her inner hero, guided by the wizard—and one very determined Cavachon.

Millie's front legs shuffle forward—right, l-e-f-t, right, left—while her back legs awkwardly catch up. She moves like a toddler testing new shoes, each step a wobbling experiment.

Henry, satisfied with his coaching masterpiece, trots ahead, tail wagging like a conductor's baton.

Millie hesitates, but Henry turns and barks over his shoulder as if to say, "Keep up, rookie!" Then, with the precision of a master tactician, he bolts toward Millie's prized possession: her orange tennis ball.

Now, let me tell you, there is no greater motivator for a Retriever than the sight of a pint-sized fluffball making a move on her treasure. Never mind that Henry's mouth is about the size of a Swedish meatball and has no chance of wrapping around that fuzzy orb. Logic has left the building. This is not the time for careful reasoning. This is war—orange fuzzball war—and Millie will not lose.

Millie picks up speed, her steps becoming surer, steadier. First a cautious walk, then a trot, and finally—a gallop! Snow kicks up behind her as the golden blur barrels after Henry, her orange tennis ball back in sight and her spirit soaring.

I watch from the sidelines, but I can't help feeling a mix of pride and awe. What I see is not just a dog with a new leg—I see a beating heart refusing to quit, a spirit that refuses to settle, and a determination to let her best self shine through.

What Derrick covered isn't a flaw or a failure. It's just a scratch on the surface of a masterpiece.

Epilogue

Through a friend, I contacted Derrick and sent him a copy of my first book, *The Dog Park Massacre: A collection of fun and heartwarming stories from Keke's Guide to Training Your Human.* I received back a Wizard of Paws squeaky ball, a dog biscuit, and a note thanking me for the book.

Thank you, Derrick, for the swag. But more importantly, thank you for seeing the true nature of all God's creatures. Even the cats.

Tempus Fugit

Time's a-runnin' but life's a beach

Have you ever noticed how much humans fuss over age? You're always trying to disguise it like it's a big secret. When you're young, you want to look older; when you're older, you want to look younger. And the time you pour into this grand charade? It's staggering.

Imagine if even a smidge of that fortune went to solving real problems—like ensuring your dog's bed is fluffy enough. I'm not talking about some pancake-thin cushion masquerading as comfort. I mean cloud-level, sink-right-in luxury. Priorities, people.

Smoke and mirrors

And what's the deal with all the mirrors scattered around our home? Every time you pass one, you puff yourself up like a peacock on pink cocaine. Seriously, do you even know what you look like?

Here's the kicker: you don't, because as soon as you spot your reflection, you morph. You smile, you frown, you tilt your head to find that "perfect" angle. It's like watching a one-person audition reel. Spoiler alert: you never catch what the rest of us see.

Meanwhile, we dogs are studying you all the time. Trust me, if you ever observed yourself like we do, you'd probably rethink a few choices. Or at least stop doing that weird thing with your eyebrows.

And please, don't get me started on the countless hours you spend preening in the bathroom while I wait for my morning walk. It's like you think David Copperfield is going to swoop down while you're in there and transform you into Shakira in a puff of smoke.

To be honest, I don't really want to know the details of what goes on behind those closed doors. All I know is you come out smelling like an artificial garden, fruit grove, and Lysol factory rolled into one. I don't know who finds this mélange d'odeurs appealing, but please don't strap me in roller skates—the blowback from my sneezing fit would send me hurtling into the next room.

And by the time you finish applying makeup, you have more layers than a Viennese Torte. Just skip the harsh chemicals, mon amour. You're much more beautiful au naturel.

But age concealment extends beyond the boudoir. (By the way, that's French for "a place to sulk." Really. Look it up.) An even more significant investment of time and money goes into your closet. Humans equate youth with body image, so they dress in slimming colors and awkward fabrics until they resemble a black poodle with a bad haircut.

And it's all so pointless. I like my pups to have a little meat on their bones, like a Swiss Mountain Dog with a shaggy haircut and a few chins. Not as many as a Shar Pei, but it's so much better to let nature take her course, don't you think?

***

The other day, we had a family outing at the beach. Foaming waves dared to climb the sandy shore until I barked at them and gave chase—then they retreated into the ocean.

There were all sorts of people, from toddling babies to sprinting teenagers to grizzled old men with walkers. Yet they were each enjoying the glorious sunshine and restorative waters in their own way.

All except this one forty-something couple. Their body language exuded indifference from the moment they emerged from their red sports car.

His face was impossible to read beneath his white Under Armor cap, dark Ray Bans, and black beard, two shades darker than his hair.

She wore red lipstick as dark as the ocean on a cloudy night, a black one-piece slimming swimsuit, and high-heeled sandals as impossible to walk in as a midnight tide. Her wide-brimmed hat cast a shadow like a parasol over her lily-white body, and she was dripping in an ocean of jewelry that sparkled like sea glass. Her face was smoothed to an unnatural calm, like beach sand pressed too hard underfoot.

Nearby, I watched an older couple holding hands as they waded into the surf, each gathering strength and balance from their partner as the swell tried to loosen their resolve. At one point, a particularly large wave gathered foam as it rushed toward them. Anticipating the impact, the elderly gentleman stepped in front of his other half to protect her from the oncoming freight train. I think if it had been a real locomotive, he'd have done the same.

But he was no match for the frothing engine. The wave broke as it reached him, sending him toppling into his lady and covering them both with the rushing sluice of water. I held my breath until a few seconds later, their heads emerged from the foamy surface, mouths sucking air, faces alight as they wiped the water from their eyes and broke into peals of laughter. The gentleman took a sidelong glance to check for another bubbling behemoth before planting a salty kiss on his partner, followed by childish giggles as she returned the affectionate display.

I thought about the younger couple I had seen earlier and wanted to tell them, "See? Old age might not be so bad, after all."

Are You Ready for Sweet Little Teddy?
(Part 1)

Ay Chihuahua Caramba!

"Watch me snag some turkey," I told my friend Buddy. Buddy is a Havanese from the next block, about as tall as me but larger in girth. He stayed at our house one day while his human visited a sick friend.

Buddy and I sat on the floor at the edge of the kitchen, watching Daddy at the counter as he prepared a sandwich from sliced turkey. The aroma dangled before us like a ribbon of melted cheese—warm, gooey, and impossible to ignore.

I stared at him, concentrating. After a minute, Daddy glanced at me, then did a double-take. His eyes met mine for several seconds, then he said, "Keke, did I forget to give you a Chicken Chip when you did your business outside?"

He grabbed the bag of crunchy wafers from the counter and started to remove one, then shook his head and looked at me again. "Maybe some turkey would make a nice change of pace?"

He smiled, broke off a piece of sliced turkey, and extended it to me.

I accepted it slowly, never breaking eye contact, chewing with the deliberate intensity of a canine calculating her next move.

Daddy blinked. Then, as if pulled by unseen strings, he turned. "Where are my manners?" he muttered, tearing off another piece of turkey and handing it over to Buddy.

Buddy swallowed his treat in one gulp, then gawked at me. "How did you do that?"

I shook my head. "I don't know exactly—I just have to stare at him and think about food, and he offers me some. But this is the first time I got him to share with someone else."

Buddy screwed up his face in concentration and fixed Daddy with an intense stare. Buddy's lips moved slightly, like he was whispering a spell.

Nothing.

He sighed. "I wish I could do that." Then his expression brightened. "That reminds me. Cats have this ancient power, you know. They can make humans do whatever they want just by purring at a certain frequency—it's called Purr-ceptual Manipulation. One minute, a human is thinking about important things, like kibble sales, and the next, they're running off to buy luxury pillows for the cat."

"Wow," I said, tilting my head. "I always wondered why humans kept cats around. That actually makes sense."

* * *

A little later, our neighbors Teddy and Tripod stopped by.

Teddy's not a friendly dog. He may be Chihuahua-sized, but he's all T-Rex attitude—growling and snapping like he's auditioning for Jurassic Bark.

Buddy and I tensed as Teddy strutted closer. I took a step back, then another, then—nope!—I launched myself onto the couch and scrambled up the backrest, perching safely above the danger zone. Teddy might have a big attitude, but last I checked, he couldn't fly.

Tripod is Teddy's human. Her real name is Christine, but we dogs around the neighborhood call her "Tripod" because she never goes anywhere without her third leg—a wooden cane that thumps loudly as she moves.

"Don't worry, Keke," Tripod crooned.

Clump. Shuffle-shuffle. Clump. Shuffle-shuffle.

Before I could protest, she plucked me from my high ground and held me like a baby. "Come play with Teddy," she cooed.

Tripod has a blind spot the size of a Great Dane when it comes to Teddy. She showers him with praise and treats, convinced he prances above the puddles—when really, he's the one making them.

I trembled as she set me down—just two feet from Teddy's prehistoric fangs, the same ones I'd seen snap at Flash, a Pitador four times his size.

"Sweet little Teddy," Tripod cooed as she shuffled away. *Clump. Shuffle-shuffle.*

I shrank back, belly brushing the floor, until—*thud*—I hit Buddy. He whimpered. Teddy prowled closer, his wrinkled nose twitching as he sniffed furiously, his stare pressing me into the carpet.

His eyes moved independently. The right one locked onto me, cold and unblinking, while the left one drifted around the room like it had its own agenda. Just when I thought he might lunge, his mouth curled into a slow, knowing grin, exposing every last jagged tooth.

Then both eyes converged—on Buddy.

"My *frieeend*, Buddy," Teddy drawled, stretching each syllable like taffy. "What's the *woooorrd*?"

Buddy's breath hitched. I could smell his fear.

Teddy strolled past me, leaned in close, and sniffed Buddy. Then, in a low, hushed voice, he murmured, "S'okay... S'awright."

Buddy swallowed hard.

Trying to divert Teddy's attention, I trotted into the living room and nudged my purple soccer ball from the corner. Buddy followed, doing his best to look casual, but froze when Teddy sprinted past him.

I nosed the ball toward Teddy. He stopped it with his paw, then head-butted it. The ball rolled past Buddy, who instinctively turned to chase it.

A low growl rumbled behind us.

Buddy and I halted mid-step. Slowly, I turned. Teddy's teeth gleamed in a tight grin.

"Let's play a *gaaame*, awright?"

"S-Sure," I stammered. "Your goal is on this side of the room, and Buddy's—"

"No, no, no," Teddy interrupted, shaking his head. "I'll *shooow* you."

He flicked his snout, motioning for us to follow. Then, without another word, he strutted past the living room and headed straight for the front door. My stomach clenched.

Tripod's purse sat on the floor.

Teddy jammed his nose into the bag, snuffling and rooting around.

"Teddy," I hissed, eyes widening. "What are you doing in—"

"*Relaaax*," he chuckled, voice muffled by fabric. "S'Okay."

He emerged a second later, a ring of keys dangling from his mouth.

"Teddy, no."

His ears twitched. "What are you, a *sniiitch*?"

I shook my head.

Teddy grinned. "Then we have a *liiitle* fun. Jus' remember..."

One of his eyes locked onto me—unblinking—while the other casually swept the room.

"*Sniiitches* end in *diiitches*."

I swallowed hard.

Teddy's face split into a sharp-toothed smile. "S'awright," he cackled. "Jus' *kiiiding*, hee-hee-hee."

With that, Teddy clamped his teeth on the car remote.

"HONK!"

I flinched.

"HONK! HONK! HONK!"

Tripod's car.

My heart pounded as I realized what Teddy had done. But he didn't stop—he bolted straight for the living room, keys still clenched in his mouth. I leaped forward to stop him, but—

"What's that?"

Tripod's voice froze me in place. *Clump, shuffle-shuffle.* She hobbled toward the front door, her frown deepening as the blaring horn grew louder.

She grabbed her purse and rifled through it. "Now, where could they be?"

Buddy tiptoed out of the living room.

Tripod's gaze locked onto him.

"Buddy," she said, her voice sharp. "What do you know about this?"

Buddy drooped. He squirmed. His eyes darted to the living room, then back to Tripod. He whimpered.

Tripod followed his gaze, shuffled over to my toy bin, and emerged moments later, keys in hand. She pressed the remote, silencing the alarm.

Then, slowly, she turned back to Buddy.

I wanted to bark. I wanted to cry, *It wasn't Buddy! Teddy did it!* But then I saw it—Teddy's left eye, his eerie monocled stare, locked onto me.

Sniiitches end in diiitches.

Just then, Daddy walked in. "What's going on?" His eyes flicked between me, Teddy, and Tripod.

Tripod planted her hands on her hips. "Buddy took my car keys," she declared, "and set off the car alarm."

Buddy shrank into the corner like a deflated balloon.

"But—" Daddy hesitated, glancing at the guilty-looking Havanese.

Tripod shook her head. "Bad boy!"

I clenched my paws. I couldn't let Buddy take the fall! I looked Teddy in the eyes, summoning all my willpower, just like when I mind-prodded Daddy for turkey.

Teddy… I focused harder. *Tell the truth. Fix this!*

Teddy smirked.

And then, in my head, I heard him laugh.

"Hee hee hee! You are not a *sniiitch*. You are just a scared *liiitle* puppy! Run away! Run away, *liiitle* puppy! Hee hee hee..."

My breath caught. My paws moved before I could think.

I turned and ran.

To be continued...

UFOs Over New Jersey

The best applications of AI have yet to be discovered

UFOs are in the news a lot lately. Swarming the skies over New Jersey, dropping in unexpectedly for lunch in Martha's Vineyard, landing in our backyards. They seem to be everywhere. And they are mysterious. Where do they come from? What do they want?

No, I'm not talking about alien ships. I mean the real menace to society: *Unwanted Fecal Objects*.

Yes, folks, there's a new kind of drone in the skies, and it carries the potential for tremendous changes in social justice. The age of the "poopcopter" is upon us—a drone with a nose for justice and a cargo-hold full of consequences.

Savior of the backyard barbecue, or just another battle in the saga of Zuckerberg vs. Musk?

The poopcopter is the brainchild of a video game junkie turned mad scientist. Or, as Caleb—the inventor of the Feces Flinger 5000—puts it:

"It's like a UFO, but it's abducting poop instead of humans."

This drone's payload is potentially more explosive than anything a Blue Jay could dream of dropping on your head. The poopcopter sniffs out piles of doggie doo, scoops them into its cargo bay, and embarks on a mission of retribution. Through the miracle of DNA sampling, it identifies the poop-a-trator (yes, that's a word now) and returns the odorous evidence to its rightful owner's yard.

But it doesn't just deliver; oh no, this thing delivers *drama*. The cargo is released in a smelly spray of shrapnel, turning the yard into a pungent minefield for the offending human's shoes. All powered by AI, of course—because if there's one thing humans trust with their dirty work, it's a robot with a nose for justice.

Where will it lead? Humans have always been experts at fighting dirty—sometimes literally. Take North Korea, for example, floating balloons full of human waste, used toilet paper, and angry propaganda into South Korea. Talk about taking "air mail" to a whole new level.

But that's nothing compared to the history books. Long before Mike Tyson decided ears were a snack food, the Mongols were lobbing plague-ridden bodies over enemy city walls. Talk about poop-occults! And you thought "dirty bombs" were a modern innovation.

Has Artificial Intelligence gone berserk?

AI has been compared to the Industrial Revolution. Fans say we are on the cusp of revolutionary breakthroughs that can end cancer, solve global warming, and answer timeless questions that have plagued dogs for years, such as:

• Why does the vacuum cleaner keep coming back if we all hate it?

• Why do humans put my toys in the washer? Aren't the smells what make them so delectable?

• Why does my human talk in a silly voice when I'm trying to have a deep sniff?

Detractors say that in the wrong paws, AI can be the evil genie that can never be put back in the bottle. Once released, it can be called on to hatch deepfakes, sway elections, and launch dung bombs across neighbors' fences.

With all the news about chatbots and machine learning, I did some research and realized that Dogkind may need to catch up on its share of the breakthroughs. Here are some possible applications we may have missed:

- **Squirrel Predictor:** AI can be trained to predict the arrival of the next squirrel in the backyard and to open the door early enough for the family dog to get the drop on it.

- **Smart Couch Access:** Imagine AI evaluating an animal's cleanliness level to decide if it is worthy of the couch. Thanks to my hacking abilities, an override button allows me to ensure the answer ranges from "one hundred percent clean" for one of my friends to "disgustingly dirty" when a cat approaches.

- **Mailman Detector:** A security system that predicts the mail delivery person's approach, alerting dogs of his proximity. It's similar to the Squirrel Predictor but adds the extra feature of tracking possible escape routes for a fun game called "Going Postal."

- **Tennis Ball Launcher:** A robot throws a ball. Your human brings it back. Hey, why should dogs have all the fun?

- **Human Attention Monitor:** A sensor notifies humans when they've spent more than ten minutes without playing with their dog or giving her a backscratch. It makes whimpering sounds, triggering guilt mechanisms to get them back on track.

- **Medicine Disguise Identifier:** Food is scanned and labeled to warn if there is medicine hidden in a treat or disguised as cheese.

- **Virtual Pack Leader:** AI mimics the personality of a wise, older pack leader and teaches puppies "the ways of the world." For instance, how to steal treats and return them for the pack to enjoy (most senior first, of course). Or how to look guilty and call attention away from the real culprit, who goes unpunished.

A world of new AI applications awaits us, limited only by our cunning and imagination. Write and tell me about your ideal application of AI.

Are You Ready for Sweet Little Teddy? (Conclusion)

The Chihuahua Who Stole Christmas (Sort Of)

It had been a couple of weeks since the panic button incident when "Sweet Little Teddy" got Buddy in trouble. I was nervous about attending the Christmas party at Teddy and Tripod's house, but Daddy dragged me along. I resisted, of course—I had places to be, things to sniff, a strict napping schedule to maintain. But apparently, "It's Christmas" is just a festive way of saying, "Your schedule means nothing, dog."

Buddy, however, had been nursing a grudge ever since. "It's a matter of principle," he told me just yesterday. "That little rat framed me and got away with it." He'd been muttering about "justice"—like a detective in an old noir movie, but fluffier.

Tripod, Teddy's human, earned her nickname from her ever-present wooden cane. As we opened the door to her house, my nose sniffed delicious odors of baking cookies and fresh pigs-in-a-blanket, while people shouted over loud Christmas music and barking dogs.

She had invited many of the dog-human pairs she knew from her days as a dog trainer. In one room, she was busy testing the animals to see if they remembered their lessons. It gave the gathering a feeling of half party, half obedience boot camp, like a holiday version of *The Hunger Games*, but with more treats.

"Gift exchange in the living room!" Tripod called as we passed.

I poked my head in the living room, where two tables flanked a colorful Christmas tree dripping with ornaments and tinsel. Wrapped gifts covered each table. The presents on the left table smelled of fake flowers and other sneeze-inducing scents—this table was clearly for humans. The ones on the other table smelled of pupperoni's, chicken chips, and new chew toys—a table for the dogs, no doubt.

I found Buddy in the other corner, addressing a small group of dogs. "Chihuahuas originally pulled Santa's sleigh," he said. "But they kept getting distracted by squirrels, so he switched to reindeer."

Teddy, an OG Chihuahua, growled and snapped, leading Buddy to beat a hasty retreat to the dining room.

A little later, I saw Teddy strut into the kitchen. He stopped at an old table with a tray of Christmas cookies.

When no humans were watching, Teddy glanced around and then delivered a swift kick to one of the wobbly table legs. The table swayed momentarily as if contemplating its fate before surrendering completely and launching cookies across the room like sugary shrapnel.

Teddy stayed long enough to pick up a few cookies in his mouth, then made a quick exit into the dining room. There, he found Buddy giving one of the younger dogs a lesson about Christmas history. Teddy dropped a cookie by his back foot.

By the time someone told Tripod about the mess in the kitchen, Teddy was long gone.

"Oh, no!" she said. "Who knocked over the cookie platter?"

Clump. Shuffle-shuffle. Tripod entered the dining room, and Buddy turned and backed up a step to look at her. The incriminating cookie was now by his front paw, and when Tripod saw it, she pointed. "Buddy! Where did you get that cookie? Did you knock over the table in the kitchen?"

The beleaguered dog's ears drooped so low they looked ready to mop the floor, and his head sank as if trying to disappear into his fluffy chest. Tripod, ever the human lie detector, gasped. "Buddy!" she scolded, her voice ringing with disappointment. The poor Havanese slinked off to the corner, where he sat looking like a throw pillow abandoned after a hard life of crime.

After a minute, I followed the forlorn dog, who was now talking retribution. "We gotta get him," he said under his breath. "We gotta teach that little runt a lesson."

"Why don't we mess with his stash of squeaky toys?" I asked.

"Nah, we gotta think big!" Buddy said, then indicated the dog gift exchange table near the couch. "See that table?" He smirked. "We'll hide Teddy's favorite rubber chicken among the gifts. Then we open a bunch'a gifts to make it look like he got into them."

I wasn't so sure. Teddy deserved to be taught a lesson, but was this going too far?

As Buddy retrieved the rubber chicken, he prodded me. "Quick, while no one's looking!" he said. "Get up on the couch and I'll throw you the chicken."

"Oh sure, you want me to do it," I sulked, knowing that the portly Havanese could not jump that high.

"C'mon," he said. "It's gotta be you."

But after Buddy threw the squeaky toy to me, Teddy saw me climbing to the gift table with his rubber chicken in my mouth. He gave a low growl "A sweet *liiittle* puppy and that walking pillow think they can *outsmaaart* me." He snarled and snapped at Buddy.

But instead of backing off, Buddy stood his ground. "You're nothing but a little bully, and I'm not afraid of you."

"Well," Teddy answered, eyes bulging. "You're nothing but a liar and a fraud. *Hee-hee-hee.*"

I watched, frozen, thinking about what I could do to stop the fight. My paws felt glued to the floor. What could I possibly do against a bully like Teddy?

Then something stirred inside me—a familiar fire. Once, I had faced an impossible foe: the towering, treacherous stairs. I had conquered them, not as a trembling pup, but as *Dragontooth, Queen of the Unmowed Jungle*. And Dragontooth never backed down.

A growl rumbled deep in my chest, and I drew back, surprised at the depth of my own voice. I squared my stance, puffed out my fur, and leaped between them. "Dragontooth knows a better way!" I yelped.

The two dogs halted in mid-growl.

I continued. "Christmas is about forgiveness and second chances." Turning to Buddy, I said, "You're better than this. You don't have to roll over, but don't stoop to his level."

Buddy narrowed his eyes. "I'm not going to play dead, either."

Turning to Teddy, I added, "And you! You wouldn't be all alone if you stopped scheming and growling!" The Chihuahua, who had been chuckling after I reprimanded Buddy, stepped back, alarmed. I added, "Maybe the

Grinch had it right, but at least he gave back the presents in the end."

"Ay Chihuahua," Teddy said, scoffing. "Christmas spirit is *overraaated.*"

"C'mon," I said to Buddy. "Let's just try to get along for Christmas."

"Maybe." He cleared his throat and said, "Well, you know, the Grinch only turned nice because Max threatened to unionize. That's why he got invited to the roast beast dinner—pure damage control."

"Oh, brother," said Teddy, rolling his oversized eyes.

Just then, Tripod noticed us and laughed. "See?" she told her guests. "Even Teddy has friends." She gave her favorite pup an affectionate pat. Teddy cocked his head to the side and took a deep breath, his tail flicking just slightly.

Then he turned to me and winked his bulging eye. "Of course I do," he said smoothly. "Social skills are a key part of my training regimen. Right after 'sit' and 'eliminate threats.'"

I was about to relax when a strange shiver rippled down my spine, like a cold breeze had slipped through the warm, festive air. Teddy hadn't said a word out loud, but somehow, I *heard* him.

"*This isn't over, liiiitle puppy,*" his voice slithered through my mind. "*There are biiigger things at play. I only follow orders.*"

My ears twitched, and I turned to look at him, but his face was inscrutable. A chill bristled my fur, but before I could dwell on it, the scent of crushed cookies pulled me back into the party.

And that was the story of our Christmas miracle. Okay, maybe not a miracle—unless you count Buddy dodging the blame and Teddy's teeth staying to himself. But hey, no one ended up in the doghouse, and the cookies eventually got cleaned up (with a bit of help from my friends). And that's a holiday win in *my* book.

What the World Needs Now Is Love

Praying for love and understanding on Independence Day

"If you want a life of action, fall in love."
- Ovid (from Love and War)

Cold wars, hot wars, AI wars—humans bickering like
cats over a sun puddle. People can't tell a deepfake from

a true friend, so they assume the worst. But it takes more than a fourth-generation large language model to fool a dog. We sniff out the truth. Literally.

Dogs, on the other paw, are lovers, not haters. We arrive with forgiveness wagging in our tails. We come with faith. We come with hope and a tennis ball.

Let's look at six ways we dogs show our love:

1. Licking

Some say we do it to de-stress. Others think we're after the salt on your skin or the taste of your Olive Oil hand cream. Okay, busted on the hand cream. But mostly, we lick you because we love you. Bonus: it's cheaper than Hallmark.

2. Leaning

When we press our full weight against you, we're not trying to knock you over (well, not usually). It's our way of saying, "I trust you. Completely." We know you won't let us down because you're our rock—literally and figuratively.

3. Making eye contact

Staring deeply into your eyes isn't about dominance or being the Alpha dog. Nope. That soulful gaze means, "You're my person." Or sometimes, "Remember that treat you promised? I'm still waiting."

4. Carrying your stinky shoes and socks around

It's like a gang initiation ritual. If you're looking for a sign of allegiance, look no further. Lucky you!

5. Offering our belly

Rolling onto our backs and exposing our bellies is the ultimate trust move. And it's not just about getting a belly rub (though we won't say no). Oh, yeah—right there. A little more to the left, please.

6.   Raising an eyebrow

Have you ever seen your dog lift an eyebrow at you? That's not disapproval; it's advanced communication. Scientists say that after thousands of years of living with humans, dogs evolved special eyebrow muscles just to express themselves to humans. Love, trust, and the occasional "Seriously? No treat?" all rolled into one look. We're not just trying to be cute.

Well, okay, we are, but there's more to it.

The point is that dogs are experts at love—pure and unfiltered. It's our calling, our mission. You need love, and we respond with a bold, animated display bigger than the fireworks over the National Mall.

DE-pendence Day

Speaking of fireworks, July 4 is "Independence Day" in the U.S., a day when humans celebrate breaking free from the British crown. But if you ask me, it's also a reminder that you can't truly go it alone. I mean, have you ever seen a dog toss their own tennis ball? Exactly. We all need someone to throw it for us. Even humans figured this out once upon a time—your Civil War taught you that "a house divided against itself cannot stand."

Burt Bacharach and Hal David had it right in the '60s when they wrote the song, "What the World Needs Now Is Love." That was during the Vietnam War, when so much of the world seemed to be at odds. And here we are in the 2020s, with humans still barking at each other over every little thing.

Maybe this year, instead of just an Independence Day, we should try a *DE-pendence Day*. A day to celebrate how much you need each other—and us dogs, of course. After all, who's better at unconditional love than we are?

"Lob tennis balls, not bombs." -Keke

Traveling the Not-So-Friendly Skies

Womb service, pwease!

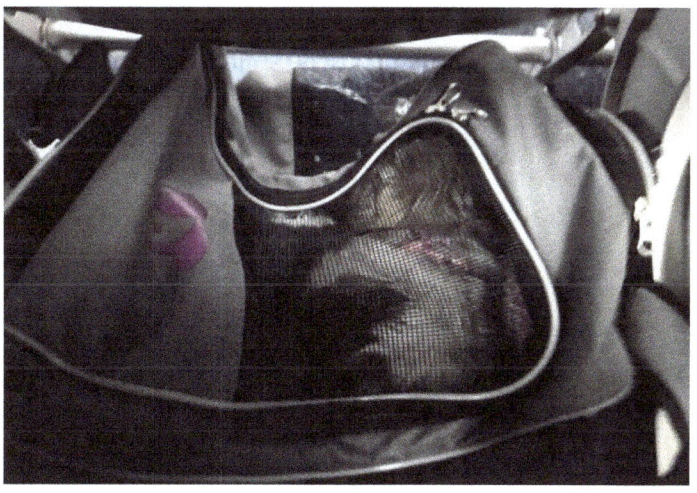

Here we go again. Packing for vacation. "A chance to visit long-lost friends and relatives and meet new puppies," they said. Yeah, yeah, I've heard it all before. Last time, it was two days of being stuck in the back seat while they rocked out to *Best Hits From the Primordial Soup*. Sure, maybe you remember when The Stones first started rolling, but my great-great-granddog hadn't even sniffed existence yet.

And those so-called "puppies" from our last vacation? Let's just say they weren't exactly party animals. One was a neurotic Labrador who acted like I was plotting a heist every time I got within thirty feet of his tennis ball. The other was a Swiss Mountain Dog with the swagger of a bouncer, sniffing everyone like he was running TSA security for the living room.

But this vacation, they promised, would be different. No car rides. No ancient playlists. This time, I'd be flying—my very first airplane ride.

* * *

The next day started like any other, with the usual morning walk. I should have been suspicious when I returned to find a chicken breakfast waiting for me— practically a feast fit for a queen. But alas, my overactive salivary glands overruled my better judgment. No sooner had I polished off my one-course culinary delight than my food and water bowls vanished, whisked away like prized bones in a game of keep-away.

By afternoon, we piled into the car with the luggage. As the miles rolled by, I drifted into a glorious daydream of soaring through the friendly skies. I imagined dozens of cheerful canine companions, ears flapping and tongues lolling as we hung out of airplane windows at thirty thousand feet, barking greetings and honking back at a passing flock of geese.

Reality came crashing down as we pulled into the airport. Daddy escorted me to the pet relief area and insisted I "do my business quickly." The fenced-in patch of grass was a veritable canine bulletin board, bursting with the latest news. Naturally, I had to pause to sniff the latest urine puddle and catch up on the juicy details.

"Hurry up," Daddy urged. "We don't want to miss our plane."

I shot him a look. Listen, pal, you can have alacrity, or you can have accuracy—but you can't have both.

Once I finished my business, I was unceremoniously stuffed into my carrier and hoisted onto Daddy's shoulders like some kind of furry knapsack. This cramped contraption was to be my solitary confinement for the rest of the journey—no food, no water, and no pee breaks. Just me, the fabric walls, and the faint smell of kibble past.

The waiting began. Hours ticked by at the gate, punctuated only by the occasional crackly announcement from the officials:

"Our flight is delayed by thirty minutes due to lightning."

Fine. I could handle thirty minutes.

"Correction: make that an hour."

Annoying, but manageable.

"Wait, scratch that—it's forty-five minutes. Oh, and our plane's been redirected to another airport to dodge the weather."

Seriously?

Then came the pièce de résistance:

"A billionaire has chartered our plane for a quick spacewalk."

I flattened my ears against the carrier walls. *Oh, for the love of chew toys...*

Eventually, they announced that the spacefaring mogul and the airline had negotiated a settlement. Three hours later, we were finally cleared to board.

Once aboard the airliner, I was temporarily removed from my holding cell—finally, a chance to stretch my legs and pee. But no—my carrier was turned on its side, the blanket and pee pad repositioned, and yours truly returned to the carrier and shoved under the seat before the flight attendant noticed a dog loose in the cabin— something I was told could lead to expulsion, decapitation, or an unscheduled visit to the vet.

As you can see in the leading photo of this lesson, I did not have a window seat. Instead, I had a foot seat. It gave me an excellent view of a dozen pairs of shoes. No puppies. No geese.

Here, I must digress to explain the purpose of this trip: we were flying to visit Mommy and Daddy's other daughter (the human kind), Kim, and her husband, Joe. They were expecting their first baby, currently enjoying the cozy confines of his third trimester.

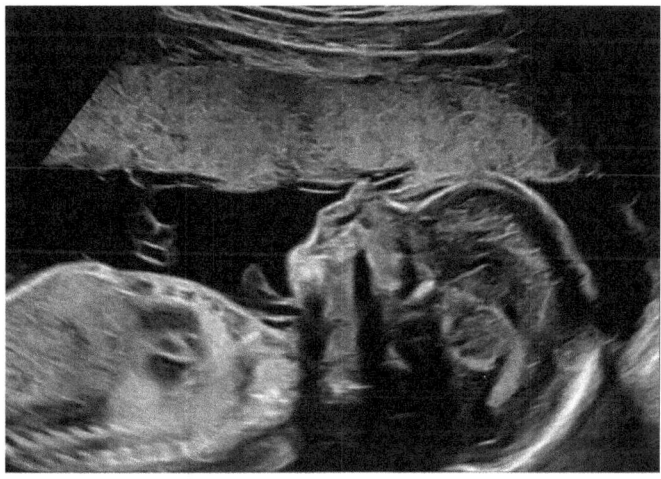

As I squirmed in my cramped quarters, I began to suspect that Daddy had orchestrated this entire situation as one of his infamous "teaching moments." Surely, being confined in an area roughly the size of a human womb was meant to inspire empathy and help me bond with my nephew-to-be on a virtual level.

Still, I had pressing concerns. *Hey, it's been eons since we had any food in this joint. How do I order womb service?*

Many hours later, the plane landed with a jolt and decelerated with enough force to push me through several rows of coach-class seats, eventually landing in the first-class cabin. (Okay, maybe not "landing," but let's just say I made a dramatic entrance.) I wish this had happened earlier—the seats had much more foot room, not to mention the free snacks.

Hey, Daddy, next time, how about upgrading to first-class? And make my margarita with bacon-flavored salt, okay? Heavy on the bacon.

The trip reminded me of one of those Stones songs we had to suffer through earlier:

You can't always get what you want... unless you're me, of course, in which case you eventually do.

Baby Burrito: No Fur. No Tail. No Sleep.

Human Encounters of the Turd Kind

Humans are a complicated species. They come in various sizes, colors, styles, and scents. Just when I think I have them figured out, I discover there's another kind of human out there.

We were visiting Logan, Joe, and Kim. Logan is a protective Labrador with a "don't mess with my tennis ball" attitude, and Joe and Kim are his people.

The new kind of human I encountered on this trip came wrapped like a burrito. Kim, who smells a little like Daddy but with a hint of spicy soap, carried him in and made a big announcement.

"Everybody, meet Cameron!"

I didn't know what a "Cameron" was, but I was ready to sniff it out. Daddy had said we were getting a new family member, but I assumed it would be another dog—something big enough to keep Logan in line but playful enough to keep me occupied on a rainy day. Imagine my disappointment when the blanket burrito opened up and revealed a tiny human! No fur, no tail, not even a squeaker. Or so I thought.

Everyone started cooing and fussing over him like he was the greatest thing since sliced bacon. "Look at those little fingers," Mommy gushed. "He's perfect! Like a tiny miracle wrapped in love!"

Perfect? He doesn't even know how to wag his bottom when he's happy. And forget about happy—I doubt we'll see much of that around here for a while. And forget about playtime, too. This little "Cameron" is quite the attention thief, and nobody has time for a little game of fetch while he's around. Not if he has something to say about it. And even though he can't "say" anything (at least, not in the human sense), he has something to say about everything.

Come to think of it, he really only has one thing to say about everything, and it's loud, caustic, and horribly repetitive. He reminds me of Teddy, the argumentative Chihuahua from our neighborhood whose traditional greeting is a snarl, a snap, and a string of insinuations about your tail wag and your parental lineage.

And about those "little fingers" Mommy was waxing poetic about. They are stubby little sausages that wouldn't last a minute trying to dig a proper hole in the backyard.

I kept my distance at first out of fear of this unknown intruder, observing from the safety of my favorite spot on the back of the couch. Cameron's tiny hands waved around aimlessly, and then he started crying. A high-pitched wail that hurt my ears. So much for missing a squeaker! This little noisemaker could squawk louder than a flock of pterodactyls in heat.

"Oh, poor Cameron's hungry," Mommy said, and they started passing him a bottle of white liquid. Gross. That stuff smelled like wet cardboard mixed with a dash of sadness. Who would want to drink that brew?

And it continued all night long. Night after night, every two or three hours, waking the entire house. Sometimes, he was up so long crying about the quality of the service in the joint, that one nightmare feeding blended right into the next.

So, who would want to drink that brew? Apparently, "poor" Cameron. At least, until he discovers Guinness Stout, if his Mommy and Daddy are any indication of his future tastes.

If I were barking and crying about the service at my house, I'd be told, "Keke, quit whining and eat your kibble!" Where's the discipline here? Where's the stern "No!" or the time-out corner? And where's the part where they look at him and say, "Cameron, you'll eat what's in your bowl, or you'll eat nothing at all"?

And the poop! Oh, the poop. Don't get me wrong, I love poop, but even a dog can only take so much smellageddon. They act like my occasional indoor accident is a crime against humanity, but Cameron's little explosions are treated like a normal part of life. They've even set up a changing station to deal with it. Do I get a fancy station for my "accidents"? No. Double standard, anyone?

But here's what baffles me: How has this noisy little bald creature managed to take over completely? Everyone's attention is on him, and they're always taking turns holding him or making silly sounds to get him to stop crying. I've done far more impressive things—like catching that squirrel (almost) or performing my "Keke Double-Paw Spinning Flip of Glory" signature twirl on the tennis court—and I don't get half as much fanfare.

At first, I thought it must be the opposable thumbs. Humans seem obsessed with them, as if they're the pinnacle of evolution. Maybe they see Cameron as some sort of tiny miracle because he has them, too? But then I noticed something else. It's not the thumbs—it's how he looks at those humans. Despite that wrinkled, fleshy face, those big watery eyes seem to say, "I'm helpless and adorable. Please love me forever." It's the same look I give when I want the last piece of hamburger from Daddy's plate. But Cameron's results are more impressive. Does he really make that "pitiful puppy look" better than me?

I decided I needed to investigate further. When the humans weren't looking, I trotted over to Cameron's blanket burrito and gave him a good sniff. He smelled strange. Like milk and powder, with a faint hint of newness, like a brand-new plushie. Intriguing. Then his tiny hand reached out and grabbed my ear.

I froze. Was this an attack? But he held on gently, making soft gurgling noises. I guess he was trying to talk, though he's not very good at it. Still, something was endearing about his clumsy attempt. I gave him a little lick on the cheek to see what he tasted like. The dribbled milk wasn't so bad—kind of creamy with a whisper of mystery, like the time I found an old pupperoni under the couch.

"Aww, look at that," Mommy said. "Keke's giving him kisses!"

And suddenly, the room was full of laughter and smiles—all because of me. Maybe Cameron isn't so bad after all. Sure, he's loud and smelly, but he's got potential. With some guidance, I could teach him the important things in life, like how to share a steak dinner, how to nap in the sun, and the proper way to chase tennis balls. Who knows? Maybe one day, he'll even throw a tennis ball *for me*.

For now, though, I'll let him have his moment. After all, every party needs a pooper, right? And it looks like this pooper's here to stay. Besides, if I play my chew toys right, I might get an extra ally in my quest for belly rubs and sunbeam naps. I understand growing boys need a lot of naps. Opportunity awaits!

Conclusion

Thank you for reading *Ugly Dog Sweaters and Other Indignities*!

Ratings and reviews are essential for authors because they help others find our books. Please consider posting a review on Amazon or wherever you purchased this book. **Click this link or copy it to your browser to rate this book:**

https://vancamp.info/review-keke-book2

Contact Keke (and Ken):

Keke loves to hear from her fans. Tell us what lessons you liked or didn't care for, to help us improve! You can contact us via email, Facebook, or our blogs on Medium or Substack. Here are some specifics:

Email: kekesguide@gmail.com

Facebook: https://facebook.com/kekesguide

Website: https://www.vancamp.info/

Follow Keke's blog:

On Substack: https://kekesguide.substack.com (FREE)

On Medium: https://medium.com/kekesguide (Medium membership costs $5/month or $50/year)

YES! Keke has merch!!!

You can buy Keke's Guide merchandise at the following online store. Take Keke with you wherever you go!

https://kekes-guide.printify.me

Keke's Guide Low Profile Bas...   The Dog Park Massacre Unis...   The Dog Park Massacre Acc...   Keke's Guide Unisex Jersey S...

Keke's Guide to Training Your...   Keke's Guide to Training Your...   Keke's Guide Apron